Cracking the Code

A Practical Guide to Better
Communications

GABRIELA GLETTE
SJ DE LAGARDE

Original title: Cracking the Code, a practical guide to better communications

First published in the United Kingdom and the United States of America in 2021
First published in Brazil in 2021

Trade Paperback ISBN: 9798713151768
Imprint: Independently published

www.gabrielaglette.com.br
www.sjdelagardeauthor.com

A journalist, content producer, and Brazilian, Gabriela Glette has been living in France for three years, where she obtained a master's degree in communications. With over a decade of digital journalism writing experience for major Brazilian publications, she founded Quokka Mag - the world's first bilingual content site and publisher of good news stories. She further founded Balaio do Bem, a website focusing on well-being. In addition to publishing inspiring content, she also researched the impact of positive communications on people's lives which resulted in her latest published book 'Cracking the Code: a practical guide to better communication'. Gabriella disagrees with the old publishing adage that only 'bad news sells' and is keen to prove it. With tens of thousands of subscribers to her website and social networks, she continuously showcases that communication is not as complicated as assumed but that only those who master it can build prosperous relationships and a better world.

SJ de Lagarde is half Dutch, half German, was born in France and lived in London for over 15 years. A keen writer, she previously published 'Solacium,' a contemporary coming-of-age novel about friendship, murder, and schizophrenia.

As a corporate communications advisor with over 20 years of experience, her day job consists of coaching senior managers on their communications strategy. She oversees various communications areas such as Employee Communications, Change & Crisis Communications, Media Relations, and Corporate Communications at international level. Her multi-cultural upbringing and her career in global corporations have given her a unique perspective on the impact of miscommunication. She is a firm believer that positive communications can vastly improve relationships at work and home.

Summary

PART 2

Foreword

Our ability to communicate is a key part of why we are such a successful species. Social neuropsychologists now think that our ability to communicate was an evolutionary adaptation, so that our ancestors could cooperate with each other. They most likely developed such a large prefrontal cortex so that, together, they could survive against faster, stronger and more vicious predators.

However, this amazing ability of ours is not perfect. Have you ever tried explaining a complex concept, that is familiar to you, to someone who does not understand it? Think, for example, of neuroplasticity, derivatives or fractals. And have you had the discomfiting experience of that poor soul benefiting from your 'wonderfully clear' explanation looking at you like you are from another planet? When that happens, you are suffering from the curse of knowledge - you know things that the other person does not, and you have forgotten what it's like to not have this knowledge. This projection of your knowledge onto another person makes it harder for you to identify with their situation and explain things in a manner that is easily understandable to them. As communicators, all of us suffer from the curse of knowledge: we struggle to get our message across because we - mistakenly, of course - assume that those with whom we're communicating know what we know.

We clearly need to overcome the curse of knowledge if we are to become effective communicators. We need to be able to apply the science of communication in concrete, practical ways. When I teach the MSc course in Corporate Communications at the London School of Economics, one way I overcome this curse is by bringing in guest speakers to illustrate how the world of corporate communications works in practice. Sarah de Lagarde is one of my guest speakers, because she has the ability to translate from the 'map' of theoretical science to the 'territory' of real world situations. And this is what Sarah has done so wonderfully in this book.

The stories from her life that Sarah has woven in - learning new codes of communication in a different country; her public relations experiences working with Dame Helena Morrissey; what she learned from burning out - are so engaging and vivid that they bring the ideas she is conveying to life. Sarah uses these vignettes to draw out the principles of communication that she summarises at the end of each chapter. Across these pages, she demonstrates what psychologists call 'narrative transport' - the ability to transfer ideas from the messenger to the receiver. The themes Sarah covers are a blend of timeless fundamentals - the importance of trust, culture & diversity - and timely pointers about how to maintain mental wellbeing in the midst of a global pandemic.

I really enjoyed reading Sarah's refreshing thoughts on corporate communications. It therefore came as little surprise to me that, soon after I had finished, Sarah was named the PRWeek Corporate Financial Communications Professional of the Year.

Ben Shenoy
Visiting Professor of Psychological and Behavioural Science
London School of Economics and Political Science
February 2021

PART 1

Who am I, and how did I get here? - Gabriela Glette

Although I've been looking at the bright side of life since my childhood, it has taken me most of my adult life to make it a career and a lifestyle. My journey wasn't linear, nor was it simple. I had many moments of doubt and denial until I made up my mind: not only was I going to make spreading positive news my profession, but I was also going to embrace and share it as my world view. But the truth is that there is no point talking about positive news without talking about communication; after all, they go together.

Growing up, I was a shy child. Until I turned seven years old, my entire universe consisted of my room, my dolls, and the stories I used to make up. In these identity-forming years, I would spend countless hours alone in my room, dreaming up characters, effortlessly blending fantasy and reality into my stories.

When my baby brother was born, my entire world expanded. From that day onwards, my true personality started to develop; I learned how crucial it is to have a close friendship and communicate with someone else aside from my parents and grandparents. That innocent baby with curly blond hair, oblivious to life's trials, was showing me love in its purest form. A love that doesn't expect anything in return and shines through every aspect of our life.

From then on, a Gabriela closer to the one that exists today began to form. I don't remember precisely when writing came into my life, but it was as natural as breathing. I bought a notebook and filled it with poetry, mainly love poems, as romantic as I am. Thankfully, my grandmother kept my first poetry notebook, and now and then, she sends me a photo of one of my poems on WhatsApp.

Many years later, while I attended journalism school, I quickly realized that working for a newspaper meant writing about hard news and spreading tragedies and sensationalism was not what I had expected of the profession. "I'm not studying journalism for this," I thought. "There must be more to report on than plane crashes, armed robberies, and corrupt politicians."

I started my professional career as a journalist, and soon was convinced that it was possible to inform and create quality journalistic content focusing on optimism and good news. Life is already such a mess of ups and downs; why not wake up and read a news story that makes us believe in a better world? A world that is not the terrible place depicted by the majority of traditional media.

Insight: noun of English origin formed by the prefix in, which means "inside," and the word sight, which means "seen." Thus, insight can mean "seen from within" or seeing with the soul's eyes or the mind. In other words, insight means a sudden understanding of something or a situation.

It was a late autumn afternoon; I was on my way back home, walking with my headphones on, in the middle of the buzz of Avenida Paulista, one of the most picture-perfect streets of São Paulo. It was at that moment that I had one of the most striking insights of my life. At the time, I was far from having the life I aspired to. The Cásper Líbero College, where I studied and spent most of my time, was my refuge. I barely noticed the stream of people hurrying past me. I was in robot mode. Ignoring everything around me, I felt lost, without aim and direction. I just lived, day after day, like a clock, predictable, ticking along without the slightest enthusiasm for life.

I stopped at a red traffic light and waited for it to turn green; those few seconds seemed like an eternity. Suddenly, I stopped staring at the traffic light, and I turned my head slightly to the left. With bare feet and dirty hair, a homeless man played his guitar and sang with the voice of someone who learned to dance the samba in the face of life's mishaps. Strong and angelic, his voice cut right through to my heart, and his smile illuminated my soul. He smiled, he danced, it was all he had left.

I realized that while life doesn't always turn out as expected, a smile can make it sweeter. This man had much less than he deserved, but he was able to make lemonade with the lemons he was dealt, and no matter how bitter, he was able to sweeten it with his positivity. For many, he was invisible; but for me, he was all I could see. "It takes a lot of wisdom to smile when everyone expects you to give up," I thought. And from that moment onwards, I realized that life is a true reflection of what we make of it, and I started to smile more, even if I had no particular reason to do so. Being alive and healthy was reason enough.

I also realized that our life is too precious to force ourselves to be somewhere we don't want to be. I finally summed up the courage to leave the abusive relationship I was in and fulfilled my long-standing dream of completing a master's degree in France.

In 2017, after a lot of planning and being fully aware that I was making a decision that would change my life, I moved to Lyon to do my master's in communication. To earn money while I studied, I worked as a freelance journalist for a few well-known Brazilian news sites that shared my optimistic worldview. Those companies and their work ethic influenced me greatly and inspired me to found my own positive content website: Balaio do Bem[1].

---

[1] www.balaiodobem.com.br

Being far from my country and missing my family, spreading good news has become vital for my mental well-being. It was like I was trying to prove to the world that everything was fine. I felt that all of my misadventures and learnings had transformed and prepared me to meet the one person who shared my dreams and the same desire to spread positivity to the world: my partner. Together, we founded Balaio do Bem, a news outlet aiming to inform and share optimism and inspiration with its audience.

I realized that the news we consume ends up influencing our perception of the world and that the consequences of this can be extremely damaging. What happens to people who spend all day absorbing negative news? Is it possible to inform ourselves without getting buried under an avalanche of harmful hard and fake news? Believe it or not, but there are many more good people than bad people, more honest people than corrupt ones, and more generous than petty people in the world. Our world is full of innovative initiatives; companies willing to build a fairer market, and people committed to helping those who need it most. It's just a matter of perspective and being able to see it!

In one of his numerous lectures, Amazon founder and CEO Jeff Bezos said, "I knew I wouldn't regret if I failed, and I also knew that the only thing I could regret was not having tried." Forget those motivational phrases about choosing a job you love and never having to work again. I work hard and spend my days creating content and thinking up new ways to share a more pleasant perspective of the world while studying how what we read in the news impacts our mental health.

Disseminating good news ended up becoming more than my job; it became my mission. I wanted to bring pleasant moments to people and plant the seed of hope and lightness in their minds. A task that became even more relevant as the pandemic gripped our world.

Forced to quarantine and with our world turned upside down, the need to show the positive aspect of our lives was even more evident. As the virus spread across borders, the world's news channels updated us continuously on the death count, fuelling our anxieties, and raised questions about the uncertainty of our future, not only around the world's economy but also humanity itself. It brought a wave of pessimism to people's lives. When people lose their jobs and don't know how they will pay their bills, they don't need a global death toll updated by the media every hour and reinforcing the situation's hopelessness. They might be confined at home with young children, recently lost a loved one, and don't know what the future will bring; they need to be given hope.

As I observed the growing interest in our mental well-being, coupled with my desire to prove that the world remained a good place despite the catastrophic headlines, I developed an irresistible itch to write a book on the topic—a book explaining how holding on to a positive mindset improves our lives.

Sometimes the best things happen when we least expect it. While on vacation, talking to my sister-in-law Sarah de Lagarde - a global head of communications at a large company - I found out that she also wanted to write a book about the power of positive communication. Rather than competing with my views, hers were complementary as she focused on her experience in the corporate environment. It was as if the world was permitting me to take my idea forward; I wasn't the only one who realized the relevance of good news and that creating a more warm and welcoming work environment could be achieved through communication.

Despite being from different backgrounds, we have the same conviction that the world changed over the past years. The corporate environment needs to change and so does our relationship with the media. We need to understand the power of communication and that with simple behavioral changes, we can transform our relationships, whether personal or professional, for the better. It is all a matter of dialogue.

The most surprising thing is that we wrote this book, despite (or because) of our different cultures. I'm Brazilian; she's half Dutch, half German - together we have an extensive collection of professional and personal experiences. A mixture of practice and theory, questions and certainties, desires, and ramblings. But we both are confident that, by presenting the importance of a more optimistic and welcoming attitude, we will contribute to creating a better world and help others build more prosperous relationships and more human work environments.

Chapter 1

We are what we consume: how the news impacts our mental health

Do you remember the last time you received bad news? Although we can classify negative information into various categories, all of them, even at different levels, have the power to destabilize us. The car fine that lands on your doorstep, the long-awaited trip that gets canceled, the rejection of a work proposal, the death of a loved one. These are just a few examples to demonstrate how negative news can affect us. After all, no one is unmoved by rejection, the cancellation of a meticulously-planned trip, or the death of a close relative. We are full of expectations, and as much as we know how to deal with frustration, news like this can plant the seed of pessimism and negativity at our core. Luckily, human beings are highly resilient and have an undeniable ability to reinvent themselves, even when facing the greatest adversities.

However, we must not forget that the opposite is also true! How great does it feel to receive good news? Close your eyes and imagine the following situation: you wake up with the alarm clock, switch your phone out of airplane mode to check notifications, and discover that the company shares you purchased are now worth double, that your team at work finally closed that deal, or that your son has been accepted into the college of his choice. We might still have countless problems to solve and demands to manage, but everything seems more straightforward, the world a fairer place, and our ideal future finally seems to draw closer.

I used these simple, everyday examples to introduce the brain plasticity theory, researched by the

American neuroscientist Michael Merzenich[2]. In the 1980s, he published a pioneering study stating that people's brains change according to the environment they find themselves in throughout their lives. In other words, the nervous system is prepared to change according to our experiences, needs, stimuli, and the environment in which we evolve.

On the one hand, this is remarkable, as it is precisely this neuroplasticity that allows the brain to be malleable, to compensate for injuries and traumas suffered. However, on the other hand, this brain capacity also makes us more impressionable than we would ever imagine and highlights that we are responsible for our personal mental health and need to be aware of what impacts it adversely.

Today, an average person consumes as much information on a daily basis as their ancestors in the Middle Ages did over a lifetime. There are infinite amounts of data, so much, that our brain can hardly absorb it all, and, unfortunately, the vast majority is negative news in the form of essential information and sensationalism. And so we spend our days consuming unpleasant facts and tragedies that are replicated hundreds of times across a multitude of media outlets peddling conspiracy theories claiming that the world has no direction.

It turns out that this continuous flow of sensationalised news creates a cycle of endless repetition of negativity, which impacts our worldview and the actual plasticity of our brain as we are conditioned to believe what we read.

In 2019, a group of researchers from the University of California published a study in the scientific journal

2   https://www.ted.com/talks/
michael_merzenich_growing_evidence_of_brain_plasticity

Science Advices, stating that overconsumption of negative news can damage people's mental health in the short and long term[3]. According to the study, "exposure to mass violence events in the media can feed a cycle of anguish," daily consumption of bad news leads to a damaging cycle of sadness, fatigue, and distress.

Having tested 4,165 volunteers in the United States, the study concluded that overexposure to negative news should be viewed as a public health problem, as it has potential implications for the mental - and sometimes physical - health of thousands of people.

According to the authors[4], the situation is even more critical when we experience collective trauma, such as terrorist attacks, natural disasters, and the coronavirus pandemic. In cases like these, the media usually goes into 24-hour news cycles and repeats the same news endlessly, creating a state of permanent tension in people's lives, particularly for those who start to follow the reports obsessively.

It was the first time that researchers studied the impact of harmful information consumption empirically. "Our study is unique as it is the first to demonstrate that repetitive exposure to events of mass violence, over time, causes significant stress in a large portion of the population," explained one of the authors, psychologist Rebecca Thompson. In the same study, however, 88% of respondents reported that the feeling of having a "good morning" was prolonged after reading positive news.

You don't have to look far to confirm this intrinsic characteristic of journalism. At the beginning of the

---

[3] Source: advances.sciencemag.org, 7 Apr 2019

[4] Rebecca R. Thompson, Nickolas M. Jones, E. Alison Holman and Roxane Cohen Silver.

coronavirus pandemic, all media, including radio, television, newspapers, and websites, reported exclusively on the topic. A quick Google search reveals more than 4 million results for the term "coronavirus."

I am not dismissing the importance of this pandemic, nor am I defending disinformation. However, we need to discuss the relevance of certain news stories and understand how quantity is different from quality. We can and must inform ourselves wisely but how? Polish sociologist Zygmunt Bauman, known worldwide for his postmodern society's net vision, has left a rich legacy of thoughts for humanity. When talking about our fragmented life, he explains that we currently have access to all data; however, we don't know what to do with it.

According to Bauman, we are drowning in information and are perpetually hungry for insights since we do not have time to absorb and transform all different data points at our disposal into knowledge. We consume without learning, and we read a piece of news that has been reposted multiple times without even knowing how to state its relevance. It is cacophony in its most perfect definition.

Understanding that we are experiencing the greatest pandemic of the century and how this will have social and economic implications for humanity's future is essential. We rely on the media to give us clarity. Being aware of the latest developments and knowing what to do to avoid contagion and support the people around us is crucial. However, updating the death toll every 5 minutes is compulsive, misleading, and furthers fear mongering and sensationalism.

Applying the theory of neuroplasticity

Since we are already aware of the harm excessive consumption of negative news can have on our mental health, how can we ensure that we are not drowning in sensationalist information presented by the traditional media? Michael Merzenich has already provided an alternative: applying the brain plasticity concept in our everyday life.

If plasticity is the brain's ability to adapt to changes through the nervous system, we can reframe our mindset through experiences, changing our outlook, and by mindfully choosing what news and information we consume.

In other words, the brain can be trained to think in specific ways. Neurons can transmit information using several different types of neuro paths. Interestingly, these paths follow patterns, which can be changed through neuroplasticity. And this remodeling can be done through cognitive thought patterns, a change in experiences, emotions, and behaviors that involve one's personal needs, and even the environment in which the individual lives. We are the result of the lifestyle we lead, the people we live with, the work environment we evolve in, and, last but not least, the information we consume.

Through this sum of factors, plasticity allows the set up of new paths between neurons (synapses), completely changing the network of connections in the process. At first, this theory was developed to understand the human brain's ability to reinvent itself, especially when it suffers an injury. For example, if a person loses his vision, his other senses will sharpen to compensate for the loss.

You don't have to be a scientist to be fascinated by this theory and the infinite ability that the brain has to adapt to changing circumstances. Neuroplasticity is a skill we are born with but has long been ignored. The truth is that we insist on being a mere spectator and passive observers of our life and are, relegating and, often, underestimating the fact that our life is a direct result of our actions and decisions.

But the good news is that neuroplasticity is a skill that can not only be learned, but it is also directly linked to the learning process. As we acquire new learnings, the brain is responsible for storing additional vital information. Gaining new experiences and knowledge causes the brain to form new neural pathways, creating a chain wherewith each enriching experience, the communication between neurons becomes more substantial and more efficient.

You can change your habits, home, life partner, and job, but you can also change your mindset and shape your brain to be more resilient to pessimism. And it can be simpler than going on a diet or starting an intense exercise routine; it only requires focus. These are some suggestions that may help incorporate the theory of neuroplasticity into everyday life.

Like all the other lists that will appear in this book, the listed suggestions are based on my personal experience and research, so feel free to adapt to your needs.

1. Invest in new knowledge

Learning to play an instrument, mastering a new language, practicing a new sport, or even starting further professional training are efficient ways to strengthen brain connections. Don't forget that the brain is a muscle, which means that it needs new stimuli to keep working.

2. Exit automatic mode

In a world dominated by technology, exiting automatic mode may not seem easy, but it is possible.

Have you ever paused to think about where you are and where you want to go in life? Or are you merely living, day after day, without thinking and just working to pay the bills? Being more aware of your surroundings and what makes you happy is the key to a more meaningful and fulfilled life.

3. Eliminate distractions

Eliminating distractions is not just turning off all notifications on your phone but also clarifying your choices and eliminating distractions. For example: turning off the television if a movie is not adding any value to you, stop reading a news item halfway through if you feel it is unreliable and potentially fake news, saying "no" to everything that is consuming your time without offering much in return. Know how to recognize all the time thieves in your life before it's too late.

4. Choose your sources of information by hand

Currently, there are about 1.74 billion websites on the internet, and more than 4 billion users[5]. The average time a person spends on the internet is 6 hours and 43 minutes every day. I question the need for so much information. Are we able to take advantage of all this readily available knowledge? Of all the news you read every day, how many inform you, how many teach something new, how many make you feel hopeless, and how many make you smile?

---

[5]Source: websitehostingrating.com

There has never been so much talk about mental health over the recent years, and that is a good thing.

In 2018, the World Health Organization (WHO) estimated that by 2020 depression would be considered the most disabling disease globally. With the pandemic, the prediction not only came true, but it proved to be a direct consequence of an increasingly accelerated, competitive, and now confined world. Alarming high rates of anxiety disorders also make it abundantly clear that talking about mental health should no longer be taboo. The topic has now begun to become more mainstream, and its consideration is fundamental to building a balanced society.

For the psychoanalyst, Julia Lainetti - who I unexpectedly met on a French course in Lyon and subsequently interviewed - the pandemic brought everything to the fore. Now we are no longer able to hide all our questions, fears, and insecurities under the rug: "I believe that during the pandemic, even with the busy life we lead, people were living in situations that were difficult to face and to question... From big existential issues to minor problems, the pandemic suddenly magnified them all," she says.

Once in lockdown, we lost a part of our freedom, our collective and individual lives turned upside down, and it was no longer possible to ignore our issues, big or small. Looking inwards proved the best way to cross these choppy waters while staying sane. "As everything hit 'at once', people were shaken by the sudden changes in their life. We have the opportunity to take more responsibility for our own lives and decide which path we are willing to follow. This type of situation is unsettling, but it is necessary to think that facing the changes head-on and adapt may be the only way to lead a more authentic life", says the expert.

For years, Julia lived abroad and became a psychoanalyst specializing in the mental health of expatriates - those who left their country voluntarily. Immigrants go through a remarkable - if not the most significant - metamorphosis of their lives when they go through a series of adaptations l such as learning a new language and new customs while mourning their past lives. Julia reiterates that investing in mental health is not trivial; it is becoming a fundamental building block for a balanced society. "I believe that investing in mental health is important, and talking about seeing a mental health professional should not be seen as something to be ashamed of and shouldn't be considered a failure. Instead, investing in maintenance and prevention is of the utmost importance; we need the opportunity to improve ourselves constantly, to become more aware of who we are, what challenges us and limits our abilities."

With social networks enabling the constant sharing of content at the touch of a button, we are increasingly aware of the need to take care of our mental health; after all, mental illness co-exists with its physical counterpart. Being mentally ill is by no means a sign of weakness or inferiority; on the contrary: it shows that you were as strong as you could, but now you need help. And it's okay to ask for help; you don't have to cope with everything.

The factors that influence a person's mental health level are diverse and may be associated with social, psychological, and biological influences. Socioeconomic factors, exposure to violence, sudden losses, working conditions, psychological and personality disorders, and genetic issues can contribute to the brain's chemical imbalance triggering a series of mental difficulties. In today's rushed world, we don't allow ourselves to stop and reflect on where we are and where we intend to go. It is as if we are on a low-speed train about to stop. We could jump off without getting hurt, but we don't dare— for lack of courage.

The apathy can be severe and gradually causes a mental overload that, if not noticed, becomes a trigger for a series of more challenging problems. "We need to be aware of what is going on inside us, and we can give it space and a place; we can only deal with something from the moment we look, touch, and put our energy into dealing with the issues. Solve, fix, and analyze, but also first to understand the context and then work on resolving the situation," explains the psychoanalyst.

Sincerity, acceptance, and tolerance are some of the traits efficient in supporting our mental health; according to the expert, some straightforward changes to our behaviours can improve our mental health drastically, however for it to be successful, the work starts with a choice, the willingness to look within ourselves.

1. Communicate clearly with those around you and avoid reading between the lines and overthinking;

2. Taking care of our hygiene, sleep, food, and physical activities are also extremely important for the proper functioning of our organism, production of hormones and the proper functioning of the body as a whole;

3. Better time management between work, studies, and personal life - Work Life Balance should not just be a footnote in a HR handbook. What balance can we implement so that people feel seen, respected, cared for, and not a robot-like worker

merely used to be efficient, and to achieve the company's objectives?

4. Assess what type of information you consume; try to understand what is planting seeds of anxiety and anguish in your mind. We cannot avoid all bad news. We need to remain realistic and accept negative information, but we need to know how to apply a filter to avoid saturation. When our communication is imbalanced and tilted towards negativity and it is affecting our overall mental health, it is time to redress that balance.

You are what you consume

There has never been so much talk about conscious eating and the importance of valuing what we are eating. But it is not just the excess of industrialized and ultra-processed products that are harmful to our health. I usually say that we are not just what we eat, but what we consume. It is not just about what nutrients we put into our bodies to convert into energy. I believe what we watch and read about is just as powerful. As consumers, we have the power to choose which product to buy and which brand to prioritize. For example by selecting shoes from one brand over another, we are not only handing over our money and supporting that brand but also giving a vote of confidence. We agree with the ideology behind that company and providing our approval for it to continue to exist.

The same happens with the news we consume since the media influences our critical sense and how we think and dictates how to build our perception of the world. When we give preference to sensationalist sources that feed on tragedies, we indicate that we agree with that perspective and give our consent for these companies to continue to publish those types of stories.

From the moment that, out of the six hours on average that we spend on the internet per day, we no longer select with full awareness what our sources of information and news will be; we are unconsciously saying that our time does not matter and what we consume does not matter either. When we mindlessly absorb information with no critical sense, we put ourselves in a passive position and neglect what makes us human beings: having the capacity of self-reflection and losing our most precious currency - time. However, worse than not carefully curating what we consume is sharing this endless negative stream of news stories with our peers. Groups on WhatsApp and Facebook have mushroomed at the start of the pandemic as we tried to adapt to imposed curfews and lockdowns and we have been proficient at sharing scaremongering articles to our friends and families. Newspapers and magazines, online articles and broadcast stations have further perpetuated the cycle of negativity. How often do we see news platforms prioritizing good news over bad news? How often do we read about people overcoming hardship? How often do we view articles that offer constructive reflections on life? Not as often as we read about tragedies, fake news, and current affairs.

How often do our phones ping with a good news alert, showcasing one of the countless incredible initiatives going on in the world? While we are encouraging this endless cycle of negativity and spreading disaster stories by clicking on those screaming headlines, many people dedicate their lives and careers to building positive initiatives, with the simple aim of making others happier and showing that it is possible to create quality journalism with an optimistic angle. I am one of them.

Every day I trawl through dozens of positive news sites worldwide, looking to curate and publish the most exciting stories. And there are so many! During the greatest pandemic of the century, many people reinvented themselves and launched incredible initiatives to help others. Young people, the elderly, children, and even animals formed beautiful connections of virtue and risked their lives, for example, to distribute food to the most vulnerable and offer company to those confined on their own.

I saw restaurants closed to the public keeping their kitchens open to distribute lunch boxes to people on the street, and cities offering hotel rooms for the homeless. I read about young people shopping for the elderly, teachers creating mobile classrooms, and an Indian businessman transforming his 2,000 square meters of real estate into a free hospital. The world isn't getting worse, and we are not flooded with tragedies and immoral people; we are just not aware of the good things that happen because the mainstream media is not interested in covering those news stories as much as they focus on negative news. Besides, the human being is passive by nature; it is simpler to read what comes to us than to look for it actively. If it is our responsibility to eat healthy food, choose to support small businesses, and reduce meat consumption to build a better and more sustainable world, we are also the ones who must decide what news we choose to consume.

Those doomsday news stories continuously popping up on every screen in our homes doesn't just create an endless cycle of negativity that feeds on itself. Too much bad news is also detrimental to our mental health and, multiplied by about 7.8 billion people living on this planet, represents a significant public health issue. If we want to improve our mental wellbeing globally, we should change our relationship with the news and prioritize an optimistic news angle. For this to happen, it is necessary to become less lethargic and take an active role in what we choose to watch and read. Let's have a look at how we can achieve that together.

Chapter 2

How positive communication helps to strengthen emotional resilience

We often make the mistake to believe the simplistic view that everything and everyone in the world is a piece of a puzzle that doesn't fit. In 1927, former South African Prime Minister Jan Christiaan Smuts wrote the book "Holism and Evolution," which still represents the basis of holistic thinking and seeks to understand the philosophy and the universe as a whole. According to Smuts, everything is interconnected in a progressive and constant process, differing from the reductionist model that understands matter, life, and mind as separate entities and entirely distinct from each other. The holistic theory successfully changed our collective thinking, and it started to be used in several domains, such as medicine, psychology, physics, administration, and ecology.

For example, in a business context, when the holistic theory is applied across the company, all strategies, and activities, converge towards an overall vision. In medicine, the holistic approach sees a health problem through its physical aspect and considers all other factors that could influence the condition, including energy imbalances and emotional disposition.

But what does this have to do with news and positive communication? Everything. From the moment we consume exclusively negative information and embrace pessimism as an essential part of daily life, we create an imbalance of our emotional system and mental health, which affects our physical health. And that is where the concept of emotional immunity comes in. But, to understand it, we first need to explore the idea of physical resilience.

Just as we have physical resilience responsible for our entire organism's protection, we also have an emotional defense mechanism described as emotional resilience. Physical immunity depends on several factors, from the number of white blood cells present in the body to the quality of the food we consume, the number of vitamins we ingest, and our overall lifestyle. When a foreign substance enters our body - a virus, for example - the immune defense system kicks in immediately. But what about emotional immunity?

In this case, there is no virus, no superbugs our immune system can fight, but we can choose to react in a specific way when we are negatively affected by our emotions. And these negative emotions can come from many different situations: from a dream that was never achieved and a business that failed to excessive consumption of distressing news or a relationship controlled by destructive communication. Life teaches us how to deal with frustrations, but nobody prepares us for an overdose of bad news and an inability to communicate.

When we receive bad news, we can feel anger, sadness, feel overwhelmed, or remain in a state of denial, hiding behind a brave face. However, if the feeling of negativity is too strong, it can become uncontrollable, and the sentiment that you are no longer able to manage your mind sooner or later appears. At this point, our emotional immunity kicks in.

Difficulties arise when our mind is vulnerable, and our emotional immune system is not suitably strengthened. Anger turns into anguish, sadness into depression, excessive bad news causes chronic pessimism, and communication failures become disillusionment. In more severe cases, hard-to-erase traumas can surface.

When our lives are flooded with negativity, we get overwhelmed by tragedies and distorted views of reality. But to avoid that, you can and should build your emotional resistance. Additionally, to taking vitamins to strengthen your body's immunity, surround yourself with optimistic friends, people who encourage and listen to you without judgment, and read inspiring news stories.

Emotional immunity is nothing more than a strategy to protect and strengthen the mind so that nothing and no one can destabilize it to the point of making you suffer from a distorted world perspective. If you are repeatedly told that the world is an awful place full of wicked people, I challenge you not to believe it and think of the opposite. The world is not only an incredible place full of opportunities; it is also an environment home to extraordinary individuals willing to actively contribute to a better society .

There are several strategies to increase our emotional immunity, such as exercising, adopting a pet, and investing in a hobby. But here, we will address prioritizing positive communication and learning to select good news as an essential part of our mental health. To start off, you don't need to read every article somebody sends you in your WhatsApp group. You don't need to engage in a debate with your work colleague or your manager. I suggest we start to get in the habit of asking ourselves: is this action relevant to my life? Does it add value to me?

This exercise may require discipline initially, as it is easy to get absorbed in the vicious cycle of pessimism. However, once you break free from the cycle, you will notice how life becomes more manageable from the moment we decide to embrace a more generous worldview and care about the people around us. Less is more and in this sense, knowing how to filter what we read and watch is an essential exercise that will give more balance to your life.

How pessimism and aggression affect your body

When we are faced with a threatening situation, our brain immediately activates the nervous system. It increases cortisol and adrenaline production by the adrenal glands, causing the heartbeat and breathing to accelerate, the pressure to rise, and the muscles to contract. Thanks to this natural defense mechanism, the human race survived to this day, but in today's pressured society, the excess stress of everyday life has kept us on alert all the time, affecting billions of people's mental health.

Following a moderate physical stressful situation, a healthy body should recuperate quickly and return to its pre-stress state rapidly; however, the same does not happen with people who suffer from long-term mental stress. Little by little, the emotional stress stops being occasional and becomes chronic. When this happens, healing can be much more challenging than you think.

Chronic stress is not only highly toxic; it also increases the risk of hypertension and cardiac arrhythmias, in addition to being directly linked to a series of mental illnesses, such as anxiety and depression disorders. Not to mention insomnia, eating disorders, hair loss, memory problems, allergies, and skin diseases. These diseases are the consequences of long periods of being on high alert, tense, and pressured, which shouldn't be human beings' natural state.

Many studies cite other adverse effects of excess tension in the body, such as decreased cognitive performance, thyroid problems, erectile dysfunction, reduced fertility, gastrointestinal issues, and weak bones.

Those who believe that stress manifests solely through exhaustion or agitation are mistaken - stress symptoms are prevalent. If you stop at a traffic light and a car hits yours because the driver was checking his mobile phone, your stress levels will naturally increase. A completely normal reaction, these adrenaline spikes exist to protect us from possible threats and make us appreciate subsequent periods of peace. However it is when it becomes chronic that it becomes dangerous for our health.

Stress becomes omnipresent, albeit in a veiled way, in life led without purpose. It becomes overbearing if you work too much, earn a low salary, are in a relationship without respect and communication, and if you let yourself be influenced by the daily avalanche of bad news stories. We know that the world is full of inequality, corruption and religious or political conflicts. But will reading exclusively news stories that prioritizes this pessimistic vision help us build a better world?

"There is a fine line between staying informed and getting stuck in a consumption loop that only feeds anxiety and stress. Nowadays, we can consume so much information in such a short time, something that would be impossible even a few years ago. And this undoubtedly has consequences and puts us in a position to reflect on how we can do this more healthily", comments psychoanalyst Julia Lainetti.

From the moment we lose hope and are convinced that the world is an unfair, oppressive place swallowed by darkness, we stop fighting. We abandon the will to do better, to give our best, and, worst of all; we stop taking responsibility. It's like being the person who throws trash out of his car window and argues that it's okay because the ground is already filthy.

The simple act of refusing to follow the crowd, and its status quo, means that you care and realize we are all part of a larger holistic ecosystem. In our increasingly interconnected world, we are bombarded with information all the time. Electronic devices such as computers, tablets, smartphones keep us connected at all times, even when we should be offline to take a break. Information overload affects our mind, which no longer rests, but if we consider that the vast majority of information we receive is negative news, we can conclude that we are doubly affected.

The term 'information overload' was coined by the American sociologist and writer Alvin Toffler in 1970. According to him, the human brain cannot absorb and process all the information we are exposed to. This information overload occurs when we are exposed excessively to the media, technology, and data. It is a vicious cycle since we need to spend much energy to consume all this information, which, in turn, is not fully absorbed. Consequently, we started to find it increasingly difficult to switch off. Therefore, we feed a cycle of stress, as we feel incomplete all the time, a feeling described by the term FoMO - the fear of missing out. First mentioned in 2000 by Dan Herman, the expression FoMO represents the fear that other people will have better experiences than you and that you are not being included.

Don't fall into the trap of over-connecting. Turn off notifications on your phone, stop looking for disaster stories, filter your sources of information wisely, and learn to deal with the fear that you will be left behind if you are not always up to date on current affairs or new developments. Too much data is misinformation, and believe me: once you handpicked your main media channels, the information will automatically reach you in a more digestible format.

If the world changes, journalism needs to change. It is no longer possible for the traditional media to maintain a model that produces and distributes information based on 'doom, and gloom sells more copies' theories taught decades ago at journalism schools. A news structure that focuses on sensationalism assumes that people either are fascinated by struggles, scared of disasters, or anxious about new developments which, to my mind, is obsolete. People are fascinated by tragic news stories because there isn't an alternative to this type of reporting until recently. People are comforted by what they know, regardless of whether it is good for them or not. Like Plato[6] and the "Cave Myth": at first, a change can be daunting, but once we are introduced to a new reality, going back is no longer possible.

Today, I've observed that several large news sites have started to create an editorial section reserved for positive news, the "good news" pages. Editorial boards understand that this is an untapped market and investing time and paying journalists to produce positive content is lucrative.

---

[6] Plato was a philosopher and mathematician of the classical period of Ancient Greece.

In my first months in journalism school, I quickly became disillusioned by the courses offered to students by the academy. A student could either opt for courses covering sports, culture, politics, and if they were more daring hard news, covering foreign affairs, wars, and disasters. However, in the four years of the master's programme, I've never been given the option to take a different approach. In my opinion, it's entirely possible to inform an audience by taking a more optimistic direction. It bothered me to such a degree that I vowed never to work at a newspaper that solely focused on fear-mongering and exposing scandals. I therefore started looking for alternatives, and I immersed myself in digital journalism, which became my path until today. To my surprise I quickly discovered multiple media outlets with a common feature: they all substituted traditional journalism to create an innovative way of communicating and informing.

After years of submitting my work to these sites, I decided to explore digital journalism in more depth, and I was keen to test new formats. I decided to launch my own positive news publishing website – Balaio do Bem[7]. I was motivated by a sense of purpose - I knew sharing good news stories would help people mitigate their negative world view and reduce their anxiety.

It is not unusual for me to receive dozens of messages daily from people thanking me for the content I produce, saying that the articles and videos posted helped change their outlook on life. Others say that they are tired of reading distressing news and found the positive content a breath of fresh air. These testimonies are more than encouraging; they also fuel me to keep going day after day on this journey. Further, the feedback also shows an

---

[7] www.balaiodobem.com.br

appetite to find alternative ways to communicate and establish new connections. If you, too, are tired and do not want to have your life negatively affected by this endless loop of negativity, start by changing some habits.

One news story, two perspectives

I have also received comments from viewers or readers, mainly fellow journalists, who have criticized my reporting, describing it as too naive and unrealistic. But I'm afraid I have to disagree, and once you flip that switch in your brain, there is no coming back. Once you realize that it is possible to deliver the same news and provide the same data from two opposing perspectives, it is difficult to understand why many journalists don't see its appeal and insist on remaining loyal to the 'doom and gloom' model perpetuating defeatism and pessimism.

Someone once remarked that they would prefer to read realistic news stories rather than pretending that everything is fine and glossing over our society's horrors, but it is precisely in this simplism that the error lies. Writing and communicating good news is not pretending that everything is okay and that the world is not facing all the problems we know. When reporting from a positive angle, I believe I am giving readers hope and telling people: the world is not just a collection of catastrophes.

However, all the theories, experiences, and scientific research that I will quote in this book might not be sufficient to convince. Therefore, I decided to empirically show how it is possible to present two perspectives for the same news story.

News story One

Negative outlook: London hospitals receive 'continuous tsunami' from patients[8]

London public hospitals face a "continuous tsunami" of coronavirus patients, while they must act with an "unprecedented" shortage of professionals because many are sick, said one of the British National Health Service directors.

Despite a massive increase in their ability to receive patients in intensive care units in recent weeks, hospitals in the capital report "an explosion" in the number of "critically ill patients, a kind of continuous tsunami," said NHS Chris Hopson (UK SUS) on BBC public radio.

Positive outlook: Coronavirus: 4,500 retired doctors and nurses have abdicated their retirement to help the UK health system[9]

The health secretary said 4,500 retired health workers have signed up to help fight the UK's coronavirus pandemic.

This decision follows on from the NHS England's deal with independent hospitals to provide 20,000 fully qualified employees and a further 8,000 hospital beds. The NHS will also have access to an additional 1,200 respirators and other intensive care facilities as the coronavirus crisis intensifies.

Analysis

---

[8] Source: www.g1.com.br, 26/03/2020

[9] Source: www.news.sky.com, 22/03/2020

When reporting the collapse in the UK health system, G1 preferred to show chaos and sensationalism. Using expressions like 'continuous tsunami' and 'unprecedented,' the writers of the first article create a sense of fear, scarcity, and lack of control. It leads a reader to believe that there is little hope remaining and takes away the possibility to build a better world.

On the other hand, SkyNews decided to highlight citizenship and citizens' joint effort in the face of the greatest pandemic of the century. By showing that about 4,500 retired health professionals gave up their retirement to help fight the coronavirus, the media outlet motivates readers, who, despite the uncertainties, feels reassured that together we can overcome the pandemic.

The media outlets both address the pandemic, and the challenges governments face in tackling it, but they have chosen different ways to do this. People are not born optimistic or pessimistic; they choose to see the glass as half-empty or half-full.

News story Two

Negative outlook: Coronavirus pandemic will leave 18.5 million unemployed in Pakistan[10]

Islamabad, April 3. The Pakistani government has estimated that about 12.3 million to 18.5 million people will lose their jobs. The economy will suffer extensive losses in just three months due to "moderate to severe economic shocks resulting from the coronavirus pandemic." The government estimates that 12.3 million people would be unemployed. In the event of a national

---

10 Source: www.outlookindia.com, 03/04/2020

strike, the government estimated that 18.53 million people or 30% of the workforce would be unemployed.

Positive outlook: Pakistan hires thousands of newly unemployed to plant 50 billion trees[11]

One of the first impacts of the coronavirus pandemic is that millions of people have lost their jobs. The world is likely to suffer a significant recession, but the Pakistani government acted swiftly and decided to transform the situation into a sustainable initiative. The government has confirmed that it will reforest the country and count on the help of thousands of unemployed. According to Reuters, more than 63,000 jobs have been created so that newly unemployed people can plant 50 billion trees over the next five years.

The action had already been initiated by Prime Minister Imran Khan in 2018 but had to be temporarily stopped in mid-March due to quarantine restrictions. With these and thousands of other farm workers facing unemployment amid the lockdowns, the government relaunched the program earlier this month.

Analysis

At the beginning of April, the first wave of the coronavirus pandemic had spread; with over half of the world forced into lockdown and facing an uncertain future, many felt apprehensive. As the News Sky website reported at the end of the article, Pakistan had just over 2,000 confirmed cases of coronavirus and 35 deaths when the article was published. However, the tone is set by the

---

[11] Source: www.balaiodobem.com.br, 01/05/2020

hyperbolic vocabulary used. Expressions like 'moderate to severe shocks' and 'massive losses' introduce the term infodemic, which we will analyze later.

In contrast, at Balaio do Bem, the seriousness of the crisis in Pakistan and the world isn't ignored, as highlighted by the word 'recession.' However, we preferred to highlight one of the government's solutions to prevent the loss of thousands of jobs. The innovative action highlights a big change to support the environment and shows how we can overcome crises through joint efforts and goodwill. Once again, the two sites are reporting similar information, but are not identical; the difference is in the interpretation of the event itself and how the information is framed to inform the public. While one (News Sky) chooses to use the sensationalism angle, we from Balaio do Bem choose to show the positive steps taken instead.

The above examples highlight two of the many ways to report on a news story and demonstrate how by prioritizing negative news; you expose yourself to a plethora of harmful feelings, which little by little shape your view of the world, other people, and life itself. The opposite happens when we decide to filter our sources of information and start to value the countless good initiatives that are born out of desperate situations. As explained in the previous chapter we are what we consume.

Infodemic

"We are not just fighting a pandemic; we are fighting an infodemic." With this speech, Tedros Adhanom

- director-general of the World Health Organization (WHO), started the Munich Security Conference in February 2020. It was just the start of the pandemic, but the term Covid-19 was already one of the highest-ranking search engine terms worldwide. The word 'infodemic' referred to a "deluge of information - accurate or not - that hinder access to reliable sources and guidance."

Although it is perfectly suited to the times we live in, the phenomenon is not new. In the book 'Future Shock', published in 1970 by economist Alvin Toffler, the term 'information overload' was used for the first time, but it was only with the internet's democratization that the terminology started to make sense. At the time, Toffler clarified that the term referred to "the difficulty that a person has to understand a subject and make decisions that can be caused by the excess of information," five decades later, we find ourselves living in the middle of an infodemic era.

In April alone, over 360 million videos were published on YouTube bearing the tag 'Covid-19'; 19,200 articles were published in Google Scholar, and 550 million tweets, according to the Pan American Health Organization (PAHO).

Widespread fear, coupled with the flood of information circulating every millisecond on the internet, forms the perfect ecosystem for fake news. A journalist might find it easy to distinguish fake from real news stories, but a regular reader will struggle. Against the backdrop of uncertainty, critical societal decisions are made, such as presidential elections and researching for a vaccine, under the threat of false information.

Several studies have established a correlation between the infodemic and the sharp increase in fake news, particularly in the health sector, including investigating the consequences for society's public health. The cause lies with information overload. The human brain cannot readily distinguish between false and accurate information. It takes a concerted effort to seek the truth, with limited success. The consequences of this phenomenon are deemed severe but still unknown.

Therefore, it is not just a matter of prioritizing positive content, but of filtering the amount of information you consume daily - paying attention to the sources. These days, everyone is a publisher. Social media has given everyone a platform to speak their mind and share their views. Not all are qualified to create quality and truthful content. The context is even more critical when the world is going through major international crises, such as the coronavirus pandemic. Given this, one of the solutions is to self-limit access to information. According to the WHO, in situations like the one we live in, ideally, you should select a limited time of day to inform yourself, then turn off your phone's notifications, and stop obsessing about news updates. The overload of information inhibits our ability to reason, creates a harmful environment of negativity and fear, generates anxiety, and takes us away from the essential task: to focus energy on solving the problem.

Hopefully, the coronavirus pandemic will eventually be contained, the infodemic however is here to stay and will be increasingly axiomatic in our information-sharing obsessed society. It is up to each of us to find solutions for information to continue to connect us, but it should not have the power to control us.

How to increase emotional resilience

1. Be respectful of your time

Our time is precious, and if the 24 hours a day are never enough, we must start to change the way we view the most precious asset we have. Instead of running out of time, learn how to control your time allocation. Before starting a new task, ask yourself if it is necessary, relevant, gives you pleasure, or adds value to your day.

2.   Embrace positive communication once and for all

There is an Arabic proverb by an unknown author that says: "Words are silver, silence is gold." The way we communicate with the people around us says a lot about our mood. If it is to criticize, fight, and get into an ego dispute, consider keeping silent. Not all battles are worth fighting.

3.   Stop associating with negative people

Following the points mentioned above, it is sometimes necessary to let go of toxic and harmful individuals to avoid aggressive communication. Do not let others negatively influence your thoughts and form your worldview. Do not accept criticism from those who have never built anything. Make this sentence the guiding principle of your existence.

4.   Make it a habit to read good news

If you start your day by reading dozens of negative news in newspapers, websites, and television, your day will likely be more stressful, and your outlook in life will seem much more complicated than actually it is. Prioritize positive content sites, share good news with those around you, and be responsible for building a framework for positive communication and, ultimately, a better world.

5. Invest in yourself

Stop disliking yourself and criticizing what you do. Self-care is not just skincare, above all, it is investing in our personal development through reading books, exercising, meditating, acquiring greater knowledge, and the people we allow to be a constant presence in our lives. Mental health is a consequence of the choices we make.

Chapter 3

To communicate is to know how to listen

"To communicate is to be open to one's ideas, to the other's ideas, and to what will be possible when both sides meet. We need to get away from the rigid notion of right and wrong because when we follow this path, it is difficult to be constructive. It is as if there were two teams, competing against each other to win instead of presenting a united front to build something in common"- Julia Lainetti - psychoanalyst.

It took me 30 years to discover that communication between two people does not necessarily require a common language. Communication can happen through reading facial expressions and sharing experiences, but, above all, it is necessary to know how to listen. It sounds simple, but very few people know how to listen.

To listen does not mean to hear, far from it. To listen, you have to open up, be curious, and put yourself on the same level as the other. This is true for any relationship, whether personal, family, or professional. Listening requires equality and reciprocity.

Shortly after moving to France in 2017, I met my boyfriend, with whom I am now sharing not just an apartment but also my dreams, a family, and a business. At the time, I spoke French, but I was far from fluent. I lacked practice, had little grasp of the grammar, and needed time to get used to the culture.

My partner didn't speak a word of Portuguese, and yet we managed to communicate perfectly well. We talked about everything; we were eager to find out every detail of each other's lives. We spoke about the places we had visited and dreamed of visiting. We addressed our past relationships that hadn't worked out. We talked about the moments in our lives that had influenced us the most.

When words were missing, we still managed to make ourselves understood because listening became the basis of our conversations, and the desire to welcome each other's views was more significant than any language barrier. We have never stopped doing this; although today we speak the same language, we still listen without judgment and with enough receptivity that communication is not a problem within our relationship.

On the other hand, I know couples who speak the same language, have the same values , and grew up in the same culture, but do not communicate. When one speaks, the other is not willing to listen. Or when they finally decide to talk, they forget the basic premise of communication: listen, then listen some more.

I believe the virtual relationships we build through social networks are diminishing our ability to listen. Posting a pretty photograph and a public statement on Instagram is a one-way communication that doesn't require you to listen to the other's perspective. Even offline, people tend to sit down to talk without first agreeing to hear what others say.

I view conversations as a kind of meditation. It takes focus, concentration, and, above all, presence. Communication requires full attention; otherwise, it is just noise. And that is precisely where the connection happens; when we feel that we are being heard. Is there anything more irritating than talking to someone who makes it very clear that they are not interested in what you have to say?

According to Brazilian psychoanalyst and writer Christian Dunker, winner of the Jabuti Literature Award, quality listening is learned through openness and experimentation. We can teach others to listen, but the art of listening begins with the ability to listen to yourself.

Perhaps it is precisely where all disagreements are born, from this vicious cycle of not listening to oneself and not knowing how to listen to others.

However, miscommunications arise from not being willing to give up on our convictions and open ourselves up to listen to others with genuine empathy. A listening skill that is understanding, welcoming, and does not suffocate the other.

I have experienced many difficulties resulting from communication failures, which today I recognize were not always my fault. I've had failed communications with presumptuous personalities who are well versed in the art of condescending comebacks. They have well-practiced phrases to interrupt and skew the conversation in their favor. These people are convinced that their thoughts are more significant and think listening happens through some form of telepathy, not through paying attention to their interlocutor and what is important to them. Most wars, religious disputes, divorces, and failed friendships originate from a lack of empathy, and arrogance, generating anxiety, depression, and feelings of loss of control. Because, above all, listening requires an intangible contract to be agreed upon between the two interlocutors, the main clause being the acceptance of each other's point of view.

"Without communication, it is impossible to create bonds with the people around us. Through listening, we feel welcomed and at ease to be ourselves in relationships. When we are in relationships where we are not comfortable, we create barriers; we get the impression that we need to adjust to the other's point of view, which consumes too much of our energy. To compensate, we create artificial 'bonds,' which distances us from who we are but allows us to communicate with the other more effectively. A paradox!" explains psychoanalyst Julia Lainetti. In other words, it is impossible to build balanced relationships and a more understanding world without first realizing the relevance of communication in our lives. Without it, there are no agreements and understandings, only disputes and obstacles.

Too much information oppresses us

You may be wondering what this has to do with positive communication and the good news theory which I outlined in previous chapters. I suspect the traditional media insists on using ineffective and harmful communication models.

It is not just a matter of prioritizing negative news, resulting from an outdated journalistic agenda that taps into our primal fears and considers disaster headlines to sell more copies or generates more clicks. It is also a matter of perspective. It is too simplistic to believe that we enjoy reading about other peoples' misfortunes. On the contrary, I prefer to think that the reason we are drawn to a story with a tragic outcome is because it triggers feelings of empathy, wanting to help, and helplessness in the face of someone else's misfortune.

For positive communication to happen, you need to connect with the other person, understand their feelings, accept their side of the story, and try put yourself in their position instead of solely imposing your opinions on them. Positive communication has the power to transform us fundamentally, but it doesn't always happen. Many media outlets classify themselves as a communication channel when all they do is establish a one-way conversation, where only the sender of the message exists, without the slightest concern about how the message impacts the recipient.

In the four years I attended journalism school, lecturers kept saying that the industry is in crisis. The readership of newspapers and magazines is in steady decline, and many publishing houses are forced to cease publishing due to dwindling advertising budgets and the shift to internet-based journalism. Blaming the internet is simple, but the real point is acknowledging that the problem lies first and foremost in the industry's inability to listen to their audience. How is it possible to communicate with an audience without first knowing what matters to them?

Listening is an act of courage that contradicts expectations. Listening begins with the renunciation of power, which is why most of today's media channels do not communicate, but rather inform.

The number of mental health-related illnesses is on the rise, and one cause can be attributed to the excessive consumption of fragmented information. Newspapers, radios, magazines, TV channels, blogs, social networks, advertising mailings, we are being targeted by a flood of information channels which we access through our laptops, tablets, smartphones, connected watches— just thinking about all of these options tires us.

From the moment we open our eyes to the moment we fall asleep, we are being served thousands of, mostly negative, news stories. The excess of information doesn't seem to inform us more; on the contrary, it suffocates us and inhibits our ability to form a personal perspective of the world.

According to research led by experts at the University of Bern, Switzerland[12], a human being has the maximum capacity to read about 350 pages a day. However, the amount of information we receive daily is about 7,355 gigabytes, equivalent to billions of books. Whoever tries to absorb this much information will invariably fail and possibly end up with mental health issues. The term infoxication, a neologism created in 1996 by Spanish physicist Alfons Cornellá, explains the challenge we encounter in managing the barrage of information we are inundated with on a daily basis. He acknowledges the phenomenon as one of the most significant drawbacks of the digital age. According to the physicist, the solution to this problem is to create a filter allowing us to manage the information in the best possible way and with clearly defined criteria, having clarity and the insight to choose what kind of information you want to view when and from which source. More than fighting fake news, being selective with our information sources will nourish your intellect is a matter of sanity.

To change the world, change yourself.

The best way to reduce excess information is to master the art of listening. Start by listening to yourself, notice what information makes you feel good, what makes your heart sing and gives you warmth, what kind of news stories makes your life feel lighter. Based on a lack of understanding of the concept of authentic communications, it is unlikely that an entire news ecosystem will change overnight, but improving your

---

[12] Source: https://www1.folha.uol.com.br

personal communications skills is a start. You could argue that authentic listening is an act of rebellion, a political action even, since it shifts the emitter's power (which in this case can be either a person or a media channel) and focuses solely on the message emitted, regardless of who is speaking them. For authentic communication to occur, it is necessary to be hospitable, welcoming, listen, and, above all, choosing your words carefully.

The type of news we consume and the channels we choose as our official information providers shape our critical sense, our relationship with the world and the people around us.

As we communicate with others, regardless of our cultural background or political inclination, taking a careful approach to the art of conversation would guarantee a general understanding of what drives other people. How many fights and conflicts at home and in the workplace could we have avoided if we had chosen our words more carefully? Let's start by letting go of our constant need to be right. Depending on our perspectives, being right is just our perception of the truth, a mix of our values and experiences.

There is a fundamental difference between being right and speaking the truth—the latter suggests that it intends to share unique knowledge with others genuinely. To communicate efficiently, you need to focus on being direct and authentic and not use vague statements and insinuations that leave room for misinterpretation.

Leonardo da Vinci said that simplicity is the highest degree of sophistication; unfortunately, not many people understand this concept. Why express your thoughts in complicated and intricate sentences when a much simpler turn of phrase would carry the message more effectively? Concise and effective communication is an art few have mastered.

We can also view these practices as an exercise in empathy. It is much easier to establish a productive dialogue when we are open to others' perspectives and listen to what others have to say. Undoubtedly it is a challenging task, particularly if the subject of the conversation is delicate. Our degree of maturity plays an essential role in positive communications, and abandoning the infantile notion of always wanting to be right and taking any feedback too personally helps establish the basis for an open dialogue.

The concept applies to both personal and professional relationships. How many relationships fail because people insist on seeing others as opponents rather than partners? People fail in their jobs because they do not know how to reconcile authority with kindness. Families separate because parents cannot embrace their differences and fail to create an environment conducive to frank exchanges.

Next time someone is looking for a combative exchange, don't rise to the bait and relegate the conversation to another time when emotions have levelled. It is that simple. It is an effective way to preserve your energy, instead of trying to explain something to someone who is not interested in understanding, but it is also a way of showing that you disagree with a violent approach. Believe me: every time you do this, you will help create a more tolerant environment.

Do not allow your words to be misinterpreted; do not allow for something to be read between the lines, be exact, and specify your position. That said, clear communication doesn't mean you have to forgo sarcasm or humor. In this space, a leading author is English author Oscar Wilde, a fan of irony, who wrote brilliant sarcastic literature.

A study led by French business school INSEAD concluded that the world's brightest minds have a penchant for sarcasm. According to the authors, making and understanding comments of this type requires the brain to search for abstract and subjective thoughts, which stimulates creativity.

We admire agile minds capable of turning a sentence into a riddle. However, there is a fine line between sarcasm and cruelty, irony and malice. Not every conversation lends itself to wordplays. The issue with sarcasm is the impact on the person on the receiving end of the sarcastic comment and how the listener is interpreting it. What was supposed to be an amusing quip might entertain some but might trigger feelings of unease for others. However, if done well, and in the right circumstances, humor and sarcasm can be entertaining and strengthen relationships.

Positive communication requires humility.

Apologizing is difficult as it carries the notion of vulnerability. We all know someone who doesn't know how to apologize. It is as if these people have a mental barrier preventing them from recognizing their faults and utter those simple words: "I'm sorry." We are all error-prone, and when we make a mistake, it should be natural to apologize to those we have caused discomfort.

But some individuals find doing this extremely difficult and resort to extremes to avoid having to show their vulnerability and keep up appearances, such as ending relationships. These people struggle to understand that communication is the basis of any relationship. They mistake monologues for dialogues and see a relationship as an opportunity to force their opinions onto another.

Notice how society has an erroneous idea of humility and does not consider it a quality but rather as something pejorative - a weakness. The humble can be deemed simple-minded when, in fact, it is a virtue that only those with a good dose of self-awareness have. It takes a lot of emotional, intellectual, and spiritual maturity to be humble, and humility is a fundamental characteristic of positive communication.

Humility is not humiliating; it is making yourself truly available to communicate. Conversations will not always be comfortable, but this is just a way to test our ability to make compromises and seek reconciliation. However, harmonic relationships do not happen magically. Successful relationships require the people involved to be less self-centered and willing to listen, understand, and ask for forgiveness when needed.

How many people do you know who were once best friends and now haven't spoken for years, often for trivial reasons? Sometimes a single word can make someone feel so hurt that they choose to fight or even erase the other from their life. To build better relationships, it is often necessary to let go of our pride and reevaluate the importance of humility.

In the dictionary, the antonym of pride is humility. However, it is wrong to think that being humble means being passive or associating humility with poverty. Some rich people are modest, and people of lesser means are proud. I believe there is greatness in humility. Usually, a humble person is mature, confident enough not to take everything personally, and does not waste time with nitpicking and pettiness. A humble person does not mind apologizing; they know that their inner peace is more important than winning a word duel.

A humble person knows that everyone carries baggage and deals with complex issues, fears, traumas, dreams, and values. And if you want to establish positive communication, in whatever relationship, romantic or business, know that you will have to let go of some harmful habits, such as being overly judgemental or harassing. You will have to accept that others may have differing views to yours, understand that they have their perception of reality and that what they say might not have been intentionally hurtful.

People have their truths, and the way they communicate is just a reflection of what is inside them. Healthy relationships are not built on the childish habit of always wanting to be right or rising to every hurtful comment. Healthy relationships require self-control, but above all, humility.

Chapter 4

Generosity is an act of self-love

"A Bit Of Fragrance Clings To The Hand That Gives Flowers." I love this Chinese proverb from an unknown author. It summarizes beautifully what happens to those who are generous. Generosity not just benefits those at the receiving end; I believe that the advantages to the giving person are even more significant.

If you have ever felt that genuine joy in helping others, you'll know what I mean. It doesn't take much to influence someone's day positively: a sincere compliment, a word of support, a look of understanding. Those unable to pass on a compliment are most likely to be uncomfortable in their skin and struggle with insecurity. On the other hand, a generous person realizes that there is more to gain than to lose when being generous.

I was lucky to be born into a family of generous souls. When I was a child, my parents would visit charities, where we donated food, toys, and clothes that we no longer had use for. It was their way of introducing me to Brazil's vast social divide and teaching me to be grateful for the privileges we had. My parents didn't have to ask me to give away the toys I no longer played with. I remember how, of my own free will, I always left some items in the back seat of my parents' car; if I came across a child begging at the traffic lights, I made it a point of giving them the toys myself.

My father is one of the most generous people I know, capable of neglecting himself to help others, always anxious not to let others down, and able to drop everything to help a friend in need. My parents are my role models, and their beliefs shaped me as a human being and gave me a real understanding of what generosity is - or should be: something as natural as breathing.

It is more than altruism; it is compassion; it is a deep respect for others. Generosity goes beyond donating an item that you no longer have use for or lending money to an indebted friend. For me, someone's generosity is measured by their readiness to give affection, attention, knowledge, and influence without expecting anything in return— for example those devoted writers who published books that have inspired millions; the volunteers offering their time and attention to those in need; the teacher who transformed her car into a mobile classroom during the pandemic.

But I believe generosity also exists in the act of spreading positive news to people. And it is precisely this belief that motivates me to continue to produce positive content every day, which confirms that this is my goal in life. It is not about being oblivious to what is happening in our society but about offering people moments of respite and well-being. I know that words are powerful, and I aim to be as generous with my content as I can.

Imagine how our world would be transformed if more of us would be selfless. A company's CEO would create a wholesomer work environment if he treated his employees with warmth, instead of encouraging ruthless competition. The principle of generosity can be applied to any relationship. It is about acknowledging the other as an equal, not an adversary.

The theory of natural selection, by the English naturalist Charles Darwin, formed the basis of all contemporary science and founded the intrinsic notion that only the species most adaptable to the environment survive. That leads to the belief that those who are strongest are most likely to survive.

American biologist Edward Wilson, considered by many the father of sociobiology, went even further and proposed a new Darwinian theory. According to him, the evolutionary process is more successful in societies where individuals collaborate towards a common purpose. Edward Wilson does not go against the Darwinian theory but claims that it alone is insufficient to understand individual or collective evolution. The question we must ask ourselves is: "Is the human being always thinking about his individual benefit?" Of course not; we have countless examples of people sacrificing themselves to help others.

Although brilliant, the theory of the evolution of species and the struggle for survival has always been unable to explain altruistic behavior, which is the key to Wilson's theory. According to the author of "the Earth's Social Conquest," groups of individuals, companies, and even countries that favor collaboration achieve more success. When trying to explain altruism, he noted that this behavior does not offer any direct benefit to the person who practices it, but several advantages to the group. Over time, this spirit of cooperation translates into more lasting relationships, higher trust levels, and more balanced communities.

It is not about giving up our aspirations but to see the environment in which we operate as an ecosystem. All the pieces of the ecosystem, despite its complexities and differences, are fundamental and essential. Seeing the other as a rival is tiring and simplistic, but, above all, too conformist. The rivalry perspective limits the world to territories, both physical and mental. The belief that one can only be happy if the other is sad or can only succeed if the other fails is outdated. According to neuroscience, when we are selfless, we trigger the brain's same areas linked to reward. This mechanism may explain why human beings are willing to sacrifice themselves for a stranger or an ideal, a phenomenon not shared by many, if any other species.

Dan Price - CEO and owner of Gravity Payments in Seattle, USA - generated media headlines in 2015, when he decided to cut his salary for his employees' benefit. Criticized worldwide, he cut his salary by 90% to pay an annual minimum wage of $ 70,000 to all his employees.

Most interestingly, despite many being skeptical of his decision and considering it a worthless sociological experiment, Price knew that he was making the right decision. Five years later, his business had tripled in revenue, and it's easy to understand why. With employees earning higher salaries, they started to dedicate themselves more to work, productivity increased, and with that, the company's revenue—that simple. To many, Dan Price is a visionary. He started his credit card processing company when he was 19, and his success story has become a case study at Harvard Business School. His leadership style is a real example of successful management and how "out of the box," thinking can have tangible benefits to the business.

After Gravity Payments employees' salaries increased, the number of employees who now own their homes increased ten times, 70% managed to pay off debts, and the number of employees with children has also increased tenfold. According to Price, today its employees are 76% more engaged, more than twice the national average. "When money is not at the forefront of your mind at work, it allows you to be more passionate about what motivates you. You are not thinking, 'I have to work because I have to make money.' Now the focus is on 'how do I do a good job?'", He explained.

Dan Price's decision might have been instinctive as someone with extraordinary business acumen, but the ripple effect of his actions is significant. His revolutionary idea benefited an entire network of employees and their families and today serves as an example of a new style of management and leadership.

Doing good alleviates physical and mental pain.

In early 2020, a study published in the Proceedings of the National Academy of Sciences (PNAS) concluded that helping or promoting positivity to others can alleviate our own pain - whether physical or psychological. Through a series of tests, scientists measured individuals' sensitivity to pain while performing charitable activities. The study reveals some surprising results, including that helping others is an act of kindness to ourselves. The team of scientists also stated that "acting altruistically relieved not only acutely induced physical pain in healthy adults but also chronic pain in cancer patients."

How come? The answer lies in human evolution itself. In primitive societies, individuals were more self-centered and focused on their survival, but over time, their brains evolved to make sacrifices for social groups' welfare, even going as far as to risk their own life for others' benefit. It seems that the brain receives some form of biological incentive in the form of a sense of pleasure in helping others.

The prevalence of altruism in life-threatening circumstances raises an important but poorly understood question: what happens to an individual when they perform a charitable act? Using MRI scans as one of the research methods, the researchers tested the brain's biological responses triggered by philanthropic actions.

In one of the tests, participants were asked to dip their hands in a bucket of ice-cold water. Those who handled the pain with more ease were the people who were doing it to help someone else. In another test, participants were asked to get their blood drawn. Those who were donating their blood to someone in need were inclined to donate more blood than those who didn't do it for altruistic purposes, despite the increased discomfort.

The result surprised even the most skeptical. "Our research revealed that physical and psychological pain is reduced when individuals, in threatening situations, acted for a good cause, both from a behavioral and neural perspective." In other words, there are tangible advantages, both psychologically and physically, to altruism; it is an evolutionary characteristic to increase humans' survival rate as a collective.

Be generous to be happier.

In its etymology, the word generosity comes from the Latin genus, which means to generate or to be born. Those who are generous are not just able to do good for others but also look better after themselves. According to a study by researchers at the University of Zurich, Switzerland, there is a direct link between generosity and happiness.

The study, published in the journal Nature, concluded that a simple promise to be more generous resulted in changes in the brain typically linked to happiness. "You don't have to be a martyr to feel happy. Being a little generous is enough." That's how Philippe Tobler - one of the research's primary authors, interpreted the study's results. Fifty participants were divided into two groups, all of which received the same amount of money for their participation. While the researchers asked the first group to share their compensation with other people, the second group could keep the money for themselves.

The scientists performed MRI scans of the participants' brains, analyzing three areas: the orbito frontal cortex, the prefrontal cortex subdivision, which generates emotions, the temporal-parietal junction, where charitable behavior is processed, and the ventral striatum, which is associated with happiness. Those people who promised to be generous and spend money on others instead of themselves recorded a spike in the "altruistic area" of the brain. This area, in turn, had an intense interaction with the part associated with happiness. The study scientifically proved the correlation between philanthropy and happiness .

But generosity is not just about material assets; it is not just about the billionaire who decides to make a donation or organise a fundraiser event. Generosity is also sharing knowledge, recognizing those who helped you achieve success, and being empathetic with those who struggle. It is also those micro-actions like giving up your seat on the bus to the elderly or pregnant, offering help to a co-worker without expecting anything in return. No matter how small your generosity acts are or how large your monetary donation is, they all are valid. Generosity is a sign of abundance; after all, we can only donate what we possess. To help others, you need to be in harmony with yourself and have understood that the more you give, the more you have.

Therefore, it is not necessary to donate money or things to be generous. Practice generosity by being kinder to the people you live with, offering help to those in need, presence to those you love. There is no more significant sign of altruism than giving our own time, our most precious commodity, to the people around us. I discovered that my altruistic purpose was to spread positive news and inspire people from all over the world to see life from another, more positive perspective. However, it is each person's choice to show generosity - either to yourself or to the people around you.

Chapter 5

Establishing connections through non-violent communication

Looking back, I realize that positive communication has always been an inherent part of my character. In my life, I have only participated in a handful of heated discussions. It was as if, even before I heard of the term positive communications, I already intuitively knew how to apply the techniques to create a more peaceful way to dialogue with people. However, with time and research, I discovered non-violent communication, a term coined by Marshall Bertram Rosenberg.

Through his own experience, the American psychologist wrote a guide on establishing relationships based on partnership and cooperation, where empathy and effective communication predominates. In the 1960s, when the American civil rights movement was in full swing, Rosenberg began working as an educational advisor at schools and universities that abandoned racial segregation. The civil rights movement did not happen peacefully, and through that event, Rosenberg experienced the importance of non-violent communication, which he used to solve conflicts, and to propagate a more peaceful message to the world.

His communicative method was called Non-Violent Communication (NVC) and, like his books, served as a resolution guide for a range of conflicts in more than 65 countries worldwide. However, although NVC is mainly applied to the development of new social systems in education, people can also use its strategy to pacify daily verbal struggles. For him, the key to all disagreements lies in how we listen and speak, that is, in the way we communicate.

His theory is as simple as it is useful, and it seems obvious, after all, violent communication does not make any sense - an aggressive conversation can hardly qualify as dialogue. But then why do so many people still find it challenging to apply these techniques? Why do so many heads of state and people in positions of power continue to have hostile communications and why do so many marriages still end violently?

The answer seems to be, once again, empathy. It is not enough to know and execute this knowledge methodically; you need to reprogram yourself to become more empathetic. And in this sense, the way we communicate with others is a reflection of the way we see ourselves. To understand and connect with others, you must first respect and have empathy for yourself.

Rosenberg was born in the United States and, although Caucasian, it was the violent racist events he observed around him that shaped the basis of his entire theory. The driver to his research was the question, "What motivates people to abuse someone on the basis of their surname, religion, origin, or color?".

For him, the basis of non-violent communication is to create quality connections with yourself and with others that can favor compassionate actions. What makes you feel alive, what makes your heart beat faster? This question may seem unpretentious, but try to answer it from the other's perspective, whomever they are. From the moment we can answer these questions, we can begin to have less violent communications as we start to respect others' points of view and see their joys and their pains. It is a very effective exercise since it allows you to understand what motivates even people with extreme points of views such as internet trolls or terrorists and see the world through their eyes.

For Rosenberg, the best way to handle violent acts is to exercise empathy and determine what motivates people to perpetrate such violent and harmful actions. What needs are they trying to satisfy with these acts? Extreme behaviors are generally triggered by distress or loss.

In a world increasingly dominated by social networks, hate speech and polarized views compromise non-violent communication and its peaceful ecosystem. Freedom of expression is fundamental, but there is a fine line between saying what one thinks and being hurtful.

Many people hide behind sincerity and think that just because they are sincere, they have the right to say absolutely everything that comes to mind, without the need to filter or think about the impact of those views on others. Why not find balance? You can speak the truth and be mindful not to offend or hurt the person you interact with.

Non-violent communication teaches us to differentiate between our own opinions, our values, and those of others. Notice how the tone of a conversation can improve if we make these simple changes. Observing without judging is a way of showing interest in others and expressing a feeling instead of giving an opinion; it respects the experiences people have lived through. Similarly, relations would be less complicated if we tried to replace conditions with inquiries.

No man is an island

"No man is an island." This famous phrase by the English poet John Donne helps us understand that relationships guide human life and that for human beings, living is to live together. However, living together is not just cohabiting the same physical or social space, but finding ways to live harmoniously despite all differences. As human beings, we are constantly shaped by our relationships, learning, improving, and becoming better people thanks to them. At least that's how it should be.

I have seen people closing themselves off to any real connection after suffering some disappointment, thus creating an even bigger problem because it is humanly impossible to have a genuine relationship without interactions. And I am not just talking about romantic relationships; it is impossible to have a real friendship without showing your true character; a working relationship is unlikely to be fruitful unless you let of the notion of competition and agressivity.

The problem is to perpetuate volatile relationships thinking that something beneficial will come from them. According to Polish sociologist Zygmunt Bauman, we live in an era of fluid relationships in which nothing lasts. According to him, relations are no longer built to last; they are too fragile to persist. The cause is a lack of commitment and trust, and the view that relationships are no longer created over the long-term for the long-term.

New technologies and virtual relationships increasingly guide our lives, and we seem to have forgotten how to connect with others on a deeper level. We have replaced intimate connections with distanced, vague commitments and use emojis to express our feelings rather than face to face conversations. This environment is a fertile ground to enable haters and trolls who feed on conflict and aggressiveness. Behind the anonymity of computer screens, trolls become an avatar of themselves, and through the power of social networks, they can gain significant influence. It is unlikely that a hater would have the courage to say what he writes online in person, and that is precisely their weakness. From the moment we start seeing a hater for what they really are: a coward, they lose their influence and become background noise.

We are all part of an ecosystem, and for this ecosystem to be healthy, we need to understand the other entirely, including their flaws and shortcomings. Rosenberg said that all human beings have the same basic needs and that when we connect at the level of these needs, conflicts that previously seemed unsolvable can be resolved. The magic happens when we stop being defensive and start accepting others and their point of view. It is unnecessary to love everyone or agree with everything, but understanding and respecting one another is crucial to building strong and lasting relationships.

When we manage to do so, relinquishing the desire for control and accepting that one is not an island, communications are healthier, and life is more fluid. Knowing how to relate is also about letting others be themselves; it accepts that our opinions need not be immovable and that we can and should be fluid as water, adapting to the flow and the environment.

Life is much more about impermanence than immobility, much more about connecting than rejecting. Only the humble can recognize that empathy is the basis for building authentic relationships.

How intolerance is ruining relationships

Many people spend their entire lives not realizing who they are and what their purpose is, thus navigating their lives rudderless and likely to become a burden or a threat to people around them. Usually, those individuals accumulate disrespectful and violent relationships without realizing what the root causes are — lost opportunities, rejections, confrontations, and sometimes just having a penchant for drama. Plagued by paranoia founded in insecurity, those individuals always seek a potential rival to compete, and any contrarian idea is a surefire trigger for resentment.

Intolerant people build walls instead of bridges, make their ideas absolute truths, and struggle to build healthy relationships. Narrow-minded people are emotionally fragile and need to use an authoritarian approach to gain respect. Little do they know that respect based on fear is temporary and that their words and attitudes can cause serious hurt.

"Stop eating; you're fat." I was having dinner at a friend's house when her husband casually told her that. We were dining at a large table full of people. His tone and his words shocked me and the other guests at the table. What level of disrespect had the relationship reached that he thought he could say such a thing? How many other offensive things did he feel comfortable saying while no one was around?

No matter how intimate we are with someone, it is difficult to understand how someone can allow themselves to make such a harsh judgment. This example is the opposite of non-violent communication, which observes without judging and considers others' feelings. To communicate in a non-violent way is to establish connections, relations of respect, and equality. It allows the other to be who they genuinely are. One of the non-violent communication premises sees the other as an independent being, not as someone who always needs to meet their expectations.

Intolerant communicators create their personal system of rules, establish their limits, and completely ignore others' boundaries, whoever they are. Many are found in positions of power at work or in politics, but also in many marriages. The intolerant communicator doesn't know how to be an inspirational leader; he is forever frustrated by his inability to manage his emotions or to communicate positively.

Communication is our evolutionary legacy; if our relationships are not built on positive communications, they are doomed to fail. One of the consequences of social distancing or voluntary isolation in an increasingly polarized world is creating inflexible, polarized, cold, and superficial people. These individuals are unable to relate to others with empathy.

To relate to someone is not about erasing yourself or deleting your wants and desires, but to affirm your opinion in a kind and empathic way. However, to do this, you need to master your emotions and empathize with others. We will never create healthy relationships by putting a grudge before forgiveness and taking any contrary opinion as an insult. I am increasingly convinced that humility is a fundamental characteristic of those who master empathy.

The Mindfulness of Relationships

You have probably heard of the term mindfulness, an increasingly reoccurring word in today's society, although it has existed in Buddhist philosophy for more than 2500 years. We live in an era of technology; however, the speed we've acquired through it is deceptive and possibly unhealthy. We need to learn how to slow down to enjoy our life in its entirety.

Have you ever performed a task in autopilot mode, automatically without appreciating why you are doing it? The mindfulness technique teaches the exact opposite. Its focus is on the present moment;

mindfulness's primary goal is to offer us moments of awareness, whether while walking, brushing our teeth, or reading a book.

Mindfulness is total abandonment in the moment, whatever that moment is. With time and practice, it becomes a permanent refusal to switch to robot mode and positively affects different areas of our lives. Genuine connection through positive communication requires something akin to meditation since it is about learning to surrender. Mindfulness can be applied to relationships because a real relationship does not thrive through photos on Instagram, nor do wedding rings ensure a successful marriage, nor does an employment contract guarantee a prosperous career. To connect well with others, we need to realize that "we can transform the world by transforming human relationships through a coexistence with presence, affection, and abundance," as explained by journalist Michelle Prazeres, founder of Desacelera São Paulo[13], a company that promotes living a quiet life as a way to have a more purposeful life.

According to the expert, affective coexistence is built on four pillars, one of which is "mindfulness, which involves being present, in the here and now." In other words, attention and bonding are needed since dialogue only happens when the parties involved in that relationship are capable of presence, abundance, and warmth.

How often have you felt trapped in a one-sided conversation or thought you had no voice because the other person, or the other people, involved were not entirely present? It was not a conversation, but verbiage, a one-sided transfer of information. People sit down to

---

[13] An initiative in the Brazilian city of São Paulo to promote a slower lifestyle.

resolve conflicts, but without the genuine commitment to change their point of view, they leave the conversation even more distant, with more differences.

Authentic communication requires awareness, not only of the present moment but also an understanding of the other. Communicating is not just informing and presenting different points of view, but, it is above all, letting oneself be affected, and giving time and presence, in the same way when we are mindful. To form a real connection with someone, be it a manager at work, or a romantic partner, it takes awareness and commitment. It is vital to humanize our communication.

"In a context of informational excess and social acceleration of time, talking about humanizing communication is talking about recovering the senses that move us in communication. Look at communication as a living process, and, therefore, it is not a mere transmission. Communication is bond, bridge, resonance. And it happens in the body, in between and during human relationships", explains Michelle Prazeres.

We need to stop romanticizing multitasking, the ability to do several things at the same time. The practice not just exhausts us, but also leaves us unfocused. It is essential to see mindfulness not only as an effective stress reduction technique but as the only way to live a more meaningful life and have more prosperous and healthy relationships.

When we surrender ourselves to the present moment, we establish effective coexistence and suppress the impulse of resorting to violent communication - this happens "When there is the availability and a genuine interest in the other; in what the other can present; in the beauty and divinity of the other," says Michelle.

Affective coexistence happens when we start to see the other as a whole - a mix of experiences, failures, successes, conquests, and goodbyes. From this moment on, we become their equal, we allow ourselves to be transformed, and we open ourselves to countless possibilities that happen through the mindfulness of relationships.

Chapter 6

A turning point: lessons from the pandemic

I had tears in my eyes; I knew I had to go back to France. The pandemic forced me to make a quick decision and choose between leaving or staying. It was the end of the carnival season, and the rain outside sounded like a prophecy: hard times were about to begin. After many months away from my family, I had finally made it back to my home country, Brazil. I had missed the food, açaí, rice and beans, and the warmth of my family so much. I still had so many plans, but the borders were about to close, and I had to make the tough decision to return to France two weeks earlier than I had initially planned. It doesn't sound dramatic, but those who live far from their families will understand: having to cut my trip short was like a stab in the chest. Never in my life had buying an airline ticket been so heartbreaking.

The airport was busy; you could see how stressed the travellers were despite the masks they wore. The pandemic had reached Brazil, and I needed to leave my beloved family to return to France to be with my companion. I left crying, not knowing when I was going to see my country again. When freedom is taken away from us, you start seeing everything through a different lens, and for the first time since I initially arrived, living in France was depressing. No amount of croissant or pain au chocolat could cure my homesickness.

Months passed, and the pandemic has yet to end. When will I see my family, friends, and taste that unique zest for life only Brazilians have? It's like I'm stuck in a holding pattern, in limbo, with nowhere to go. The pandemic separated couples and entire families, tested marriages and friendships. Parents were forced to homeschool their children as schools shut down, entire workforces shifted to work from home, whole industries were put on hold, travel stopped, some people were furloughed or lost their jobs, some saw their businesses go bankrupt, and a tragic few were left homeless. Yet, nothing compares to the thousands of human lives lost and the grief of losing a loved one to the deadly virus.

The coronavirus pandemic shook us to our core, took us out of our comfort zone, and forced us to redesign our way of thinking and reinvent our society. However positive you want to remain; it still sounds like the cruelest test. In the first weeks of lockdown, the feeling that the whole world was coming together to fight a common enemy was strong. Nothing like we've seen before, not a nuclear bomb, not a warmongering dictator, not even a monster with a face, as we are used to seeing in movies and series — but an invisible enemy, silent and deadly.

What do we need to learn from this situation? What is the lesson that we will remember after we beat the virus? Today it may be hard to believe, but we will overcome this challenge, in the near future hopefully. It will be a chapter in our history books, and every grandparent in the world is likely to tell their grandchildren about the time when the Coronavirus paralyzed the entire planet. "Our society is problem-solving obsessed. When facing so many uncertainties, those who followed an inflexible routine found themselves in a somewhat delicate situation because they faced something new and unpredictable. And unlike anything they've been looking for", clarifies psychoanalyst Julia Lainetti.

However, there is also beauty in chaos. I witnessed people dressed as superheroes handing out food to the homeless. I saw declarations of love made behind a hospital window. I noticed restaurants closing their doors but keeping their kitchens working at full capacity to produce lunch boxes for those in need. In Canada, hotels and stadiums were converted into shelters for homeless people. I witnessed enemies making peace, skeptics saying, "I love you," and thousands of people reinventing themselves during this hiatus as if someone hit the pause button on our hectic world and made everything clearer. It no longer makes sense to be in a toxic relationship, in a job without purpose, and in a city that sucks up your strengths. And with the realization that our lives are short and precarious comes the courage to change and cross the bridge without looking back.

Life is too short to kiss without passion, submit to a boss who doesn't believe in your potential, or live an existence that answers to someone else's expectations, instead of yours. Because in that moment, when we finally get out of limbo, we remember what makes our hearts flutter.

The right time is now.

Before the pandemic, the day's 24 hours always seemed insufficient, and the years just passed by at great speed. Notice how our notion of time has changed. Social isolation and remote working, even enforced, made it clear how our life was consuming us before covid.

One year has never been this long, and one day never had this many hours to complete everything we needed and still have time left over. Because we discovered that we don't have to manage everything, it's okay not to be as productive as before, not having the perfect home, or not have the perfect haircut. Breathe, live as the moment calls for, with calm. 'It takes peace to be able to smile,' like the Brazilian musician and composer Almir Sater's song.

He is an ordinary worker, he gets up before the sun rises, takes a shower, eats breakfast, and faces a few hours in traffic to get to work. After a hard day's work, he gets stuck in traffic on the way back, he comes home tired, his head throbs, he eats his dinner, occasionally drinks a beer or two, and sits on the sofa. He watches any program until sleep hits, and then he crawls back to bed.

On weekends he relaxes. He sleeps until noon, eats until he's full and meets his friends. He lives as if there is no tomorrow until Sunday night arrives, and he is swallowed up again by the same exhausting and hollow routine. Hollow because it lacks passion. We only feel fulfilled when we live a life with purpose. And living with purpose is much more than working to pay the bills. A life with purpose happens with self-knowledge when we understand precisely what makes our heart beat faster. I'm not talking about recognition and money; I'm talking about success - and success according to me is having the courage to lead the life we've always dreamed of.

What is the life you always dreamed of? How much longer do you need to obtain it? Will it just remain a dusty magazine page at the bottom of the drawer, or will you finally roll up your sleeves and start fighting tooth and nail for this life? If there is one thing the pandemic has taught us, it is that the time is now, waiting doesn't make any sense.

Happiness is not something that is sought, but that is achieved. And being happy is directly connected to the lifestyle we lead. You won't be satisfied as long as you stay in the job you hate, with the boyfriend who doesn't respect you and accepting that life doesn't need to be a broken car that always needs a push.

Life is a path and being on it requires courage. Embrace the chaos of the pandemic and start designing the future you've always dreamed of. You must do it; you owe it to yourself. Forget others' expectations; you are not here to please anyone and make other people's dreams come true. From the moment we decide to change, the entire universe conspires in our favor, but a mere desire to change is not enough: you must take the first step and take action.

Five Teachings from the pandemic.

December 31 in China, the last day of 2019, foreshadowed a complicated year ahead. 2020 would be full of individual and collective challenges. In today's globalized world with open borders, the virus spread to all continents in record time. The pandemic occurred without warning and shoved us all in the same boat, leaving us disoriented and scared. But what can we learn from this experience?

1. We need to rethink our relationship with work.

Although remote working has been proven to be effective in the past, many companies still rejected it, favoring presenteeism in the office. Some professions need their experts to be in the office or workplaces, such as doctors and construction workers. However, a journalist or a communications officer can efficiently work from home. This is true for countless professions. With the technology that we have at our disposal, several tools allow us to have an office 'in the cloud.' By insisting on sticking to traditional work models, companies ignore the positive changes that remote working bring and their impact on our environment. Thousands of people commuting to their offices without needing to means more traffic, more greenhouse gas emissions, more natural resources being used, and more stressed professionals.

It is high time to rethink our relationship with work. Of course, this requires some adjustments; after all, some professions depend precisely on a home-work commute. We also need rules and limits to prevent lower wages and longer working hours. However, overall it became evident that our relationship with work needs to be reshaped.

2. Less is more: conscious consumption.

During the lockdown, we had the opportunity to refocus our buying habits. We became more conscious of our unrestrained consumption, and we started asking ourselves, "Do I need this? Do I want to risk my life going out to buy it?". Impulse purchases on the weekend have declined 30%[14]; we are more aware of our impact on the planet. We avoided shopping at supermarkets and instead valued the small local producer, who keeps a close eye on all the production stages of the goods he sells, who depends on us to continue doing business. We no longer feel loyal to big brands' fast fashion that pollutes the environment and employs people in slavery-like conditions. We realized the latest smartphone wasn't a shortcut to happiness, nor did we need designer jeans to feel beautiful.

The pandemic has reminded us that acceptance comes from within and that a life full of meaning is more valuable than a closet packed with shoes. Early in the pandemic, a map went viral on social networks: it showed

---

[14] Source: https://www.publico.pt/

China's gas emissions levels dropping dramatically during the quarantine. What can we learn from this? For a long time, we've known that our obsession with overconsumption was harming our environment. Clothing brands push us to change wardrobes every season; technology giants manufacture devices with programmed obsolescence; we are continually bombarded with advertisements on social networks to buy things we don't need. We need to slow down, value what matters, and be more aware of what we are consuming. Think before you buy: do you need it? Do you know where and how this product was manufactured? Will this product be useful? If any of these answers is "no," it might be that this impulse buy might crowd your closet until it goes to waste.

3. The greatest gift is your presence.

Our lives are so fast-paced today that we seem to have forgotten that our most significant proof of love to our friends and families is being present. Our life cannot just be about work and paying bills. We should look to value the relationship with family and friends more because they will be the ones we'll call on for support when our world dissolves at the seams. While the world economy suffers a sharp slowdown, it will recover; the health of those we love might not. We must cherish the time spent with our parents, grandparents, and friends who have always been by our side. A silver lining of the pandemic was that many parents and children found an opportunity to reconnect and strengthen their relationship. Many families shared the same house but were estranged. The pandemic changed that dynamic significantly. Children get to know their parents a little better; parents want to play a more active part of their children's aspirations; siblings are no longer mere housemates. The pandemic forced us to get to know each other better, look at each other with empathy and without judgment, show our weaknesses, and recognize who is a safe haven. By the end of the pandemic, our greatest wish will likely be traveling and exploring the world. But this time, our wanderlust won't be rooted in a desire to escape; it will be with the certainty that we have a home and a strong network of supportive friends and family to come back to.

4.   Reconnecting with nature.

We have become digital nomads embracing technological advances; we know how to build a website and make money through Instagram; we invented gadgets and widgets, making our lives easier. On the flip side, we forgot entirely the critical relationship that our ancestors had with nature. Plant a tree, understand the cycles of nature, grow your own food, take care of animals, light a campfire. People today buy chopped fruits and salads packaged in Styrofoam boxes and forget that they grow in soil. Nature provides most of what we need, but we decided to ignore it over the past few decades. With the pandemic came a moment of realization: focusing on the things that matter - a sustainable planet and a healthy society.

When was the last time you turned off your cell phone and lived according to the rhythm of nature, walked with bare feet in the grass, and picked a fruit from the tree? After having their freedom taken away, many people realized that being close to nature improves our physical and mental health. It is no coincidence that many people left the big city in the middle of the pandemic to live in a cabin in the woods or on the beach. Contact with nature makes us more creative and lighter and teaches us to appreciate the simple things in life. The growing number of people with sleep disorders, high levels of stress, and anxiety is a by-product of our 'always on' society, but it took a pandemic for many people to rethink their lifestyle. In times of need, it is not a closet full of expensive clothes that will give us comfort, but we'll find happiness in the waves of the sea, the wind ruffling our hair, in the song of birds and the smell of wet grass. To allow yourself to connect with nature is to connect with yourself.

5. We are all one.

According to a Mauna Loa Observatory survey in Hawaii, in 2019[15], the planet reached its most critical level of concentration of pollutants in the atmosphere. The emission of carbon dioxide is related to the burning of fossil fuels, deforestation, and the increase in the Earth's temperature. This same study showed that a 2-degree rise in temperature on the planet could cause 25% more heatwaves, causing about 388 million people to suffer from water scarcity and 194.5 million to suffer the effects of severe droughts. In addition, it described that about 27% of the planet was at risk of contamination by diseases and pandemics. Now wasn't that an accurate prediction?

A picture is worth a thousand words. You might have seen the photographic before and after series that went viral on social media. It showed different locations of the world before and after the pandemic hit. With factories closed, cars parked in the garage, and people staying at home, the world breathed again. Cities saw their pollution levels decrease to levels not seen in decades, animals returning to live a free life, and people realizing that money is not everything. It took a pandemic with enforced social isolation to remind us that we don't fare well in isolation and to recognize that we are part of a whole - our

---

[15] Source: https://eu.usatoday.com

society and the planet we inhabit. The actions we take today can impact a person on the other side of the world and future generations. Let's focus on being more aware of the life we are leading and our role in the world. Let's respect our neighbors, be kind to animals, and appreciate the waters' cleanliness, the flowers blooming in our garden, and the fresh air we breathe. We are not the owners of the land; we are the land itself.

Chapter 7

Reconciling with failure and chaos

"It is good to celebrate success, but it is more important to pay attention to the lessons of failure." Anyone could have said this sentence; after all, every single person has experienced failure at some point in their life. But, as unlikely as it may seem, this is a quote by none other than Bill Gates - Microsoft's founder. Legend has it that the philanthropist and one of the richest men in the world said this as he joined Harvard in 1973 and met those who would become part of Microsoft, a company that brought the concept of personal computers to people. What you may not know, however, is that before he became the CEO of the multinational company, Bill Gates founded a company called Traf-O-Data, which turned out to be a disaster. To us, ordinary people, admitting failure is taboo; Bill Gates, however, happily tells the story of his reconciliation with defeat. According to him, the lessons learned from this failure allowed him to embark on his successful career.

She was a single mother, unemployed, looking for an opportunity to earn a living, and trying not to be defeated by the countless rejections she received from publishers. For years, JK Rowling clung to her dream until she finally published "Harry Potter and the Philosopher's Stone" in 1997. Today the wizard's saga has sold over 500 million copies in more than 50 languages, but it was through facing headwinds and accepting rejection that she could build the empire that the Harry Potter story is today. For the writer, the strength that gave her the courage to keep trying came from the simple fact that she felt she had nothing to lose.

Like JK Rowling and Bill Gates, ordinary people fail every day, but what differentiates the winner from the loser, besides not giving up, is admitting failure. It seems simple, but embracing failure is hard and often painful, as it involves scrutinizing our weaknesses and accepting that we are not always right. But, there is beauty in pain, and there can be richness in the things that went wrong.

However, we were never taught how to deal with defeat; we always want to be the best at all costs; we forget that the most important development is our own. Seeking to be better than yesterday is fuel for excellence; wanting to be the best at any cost is an eternal source of frustration. The difficulty in dealing with failure may be based on self-esteem or the lack of, but it is also a societal construct. Back in my school days, above-average graded exam papers were marked in black or blue ink, whereas mistakes and low graded papers were marked up in bright red, the color that shamed us for our below-average performance. The color red symbolizes passion and energy but is also associated with power, war, danger, and violence. How many times did those red markups destabilize you or even brought tears of shame to your eyes?

Some of us may not have accepted those red markups and even alleged that the teacher made a mistake, making room for accusations and violent exchanges - those are the people who refuse to accept that they do not know everything and that they have failed. But the point is that getting it right the first time is invariably impossible, and the sooner we accept this fact, the lighter and more successful we can be.

Forgiving our mistakes opens up a range of possibilities and allows us to recognize that starting over is an excellent opportunity to test new paths and apply lessons learned to get it right. Failure works a lot like our immune system: the more you fail, the more "antibodies" you will have produced to face the next battles. It is that simple. After all, who do you think are the winners, if not people who have tried again and again?

"Many of our greatest achievements - from recent discoveries, Nobel Prize winners, classics in literature, fine arts, and dance, to revolutionary, innovative endeavors - were, in fact, not revolutionary feats, but gradual corrections, incremental adjustments, based on the experience acquired," explains the American author Sarah Lewis. In her book, "The Power of Failure," she describes how embracing failure can act as an influential driving force in our lives.

However, much of our inability to deal with defeat comes from immediacy. As a society, we are focused on speed, increasingly impatient and anxious. People forget that to harvest, it is necessary to plant, and it requires time for plants to grow. In other words, accepting that failure is not permanent allows us to transform, polish what is still crude and understand that a long walk is made up of steps, some detours, and much patience.

Whoever embraces defeat is in control of their narrative.

Plans and intricate spreadsheets in Excel lose their value in the face of countless uncertainties in life. The indisputable truth is that sooner or later, we are bound to fail. Excellence happens when we make peace with our failures, stop being victims, and instead decide to be the protagonists in our story. When we rid ourselves of the mask of victimhood, we take control of our lives and relationships. Victims build walls, tend to be manipulative and feel sorry for themselves. These three characteristics have never led anyone to success.

Just as there is no light without darkness, it is impossible to achieve success without first experiencing failure. However, it is wrong to think that we can achieve this through anger. We need to look at our mistakes with empathy and more kindness, however hard it may be.

Having the humility to admit that things didn't work out and that perhaps it was our fault allows us to accept our failures. And then move forward. Because the world is already full of taboos, and sweeping defeats under the carpet will only make the room dustier and the vision more blurred.

Not to mention that to think that external forces solely cause our failures is to believe that our lives are controlled by someone else when in fact we are in charge the whole time. Relegating your life to destiny is the most convenient way of not being responsible for the journey itself. You will end up with scraped knees and moments of despair, but you have to get your hands dirty to get up.

So, the next time a plan, a relationship, a dream, or any goal you had in mind goes wrong, give thanks for the opportunity and trust the process. Henry Ford said that the real failure is when we experience a failure and learn nothing from it. Walking away without assimilating the lessons learned is the real failure.

Sport is the biggest teacher because a true sportsman starts his career knowing that he will not always win. Life is like a football match: you can lose or win, but the real winner is the one who loses, leaves the stadium with his head held high, and still congratulates his opponents. There is greatness in knowing how to accept defeat, and as we become masters of it, our mistakes get smaller and smaller and our chances to be successful get bigger and bigger. However, assuming that life is solely a series of opportunities to make mistakes is resignation. On the flip side, being hard as a rock, despite the strength, will not allow you to grow since rocks cannot be shaped. According to author Nassim Nicholas Taleb, it is possible to build resistance to weather the blow of failure and still benefit from it.

In the book "Antifragile: the benefits of chaos," Taleb works on the concept of being antifragile, a neologism he created since no term could describe a person that not only welcomes uncertainty and randomness but becomes stronger through it. A trained mathematician, the Lebanese-American essayist, is an expert in risk analysis and a former trader on Wall Street, but his theory can be used to understand more than just the financial market.

It is not about resilience. To the author, someone resilient is capable of withstanding impacts but essentially remains the same. Being antifragile, on the other hand, is more beneficial. Only those who are antifragile benefit from the blows and thrive when exposed to uncertainty and disorder. Like the human body and the immune system, we will face many stressors throughout life, and it is up to us to decide how to react to them. Taleb's theory uses the logic of antifragility to deal with various subjects, such as entrepreneurship and business, and helps to understand a simple concept: the more knowledge we have, the easier it becomes to use the volatility of life in our favor. Experience is not just about what we learn from books in school, but it is, above all, self-knowledge - and this comes with recognizing our failures.

Feeling comfortable in chaos is like drinking from the fountain of stoicism: controlling our emotions, letting go of self-pity, and channeling energies towards solving the problem itself. Be persistent, have a strategic vision of what you plan to achieve, and protect your inner-self with generosity and acceptance. Many things are out of our control, but we are the ones who choose how to deal with life's mishaps. Stop for a few moments, try to distance yourself from your failures, and notice the hidden opportunities in the problems. Whether personal or professional, large or small, defeats can be disappointing, but they are not the ones that matter. Don't let failures define your life. The most important thing is how we face these chaotic situations.

My life has regularly been rocked by chaos, and while it often caught me off guard and hit me without warning, it was not damaging in the long-term. As a teenager, I got my ears pierced, and a few days later, I got an infection. My mother tried to convince me to take the earrings off, but my pride was greater. I believed I could avoid some things solely by being stubborn.

I only agreed to take the earrings off when I could no longer hide how much it hurt. With a red ear, a throbbing head, and unable to lie down on a pillow, I swallowed my bruised teenager's ego and asked my mother to help me take them off. Facing the bathroom mirror, my mother watched over me like an animal does with its young, still unprepared for the outside world. As I sobbed in pain, she said to me, "Hang in there, my daughter. You have to be strong". Despite the pain, I suddenly understood and stopped crying, she managed to pull the earring, and that simple phrase came in handy in countless moments of life.

Occasionally, I close my eyes and travel back to that moment. I walk across the beige tiles of the bathroom, past the green bathtub, and hear my mother's voice again. Her words, coming from someone who knows that succeeding in life takes strength, and that to win, it is necessary to understand how to lose. When I think about giving up in moments of despair, I stop for a moment and take my mind back to that memory. I feel my mother's hands in my hair and hear her advice.

So, next time your life gets too complicated, and your difficulties are so painful that you want to give up, stop for a moment. Visualize the life you aspire to, calculate how much is left to get there, and give up giving up. Take a deep breath and rest as much as necessary, but do not give in to the possibility of giving up. Draw new plans, change your strategy, and improve your skills. Play with chaos, dance with failures, show that you are not afraid, and magic will happen. It is not a question of being truly invincible, as there is incredible strength in vulnerability, but of turning obstacles into grains of sand and building a castle with them.

Five ways to benefit from mistakes and live more peacefully.

Not everyone is confident enough to deal with a failure, as the inability to do so results from a set of values and the individual's upbringing. There are only two ways to deal with defeat, and if one way is to make it a taboo, the only other possible option is to turn the failure around and profit from its learnings.

1.   Have more empathy for yourself.

We talk so much about having empathy for others, but have you tried to be more generous with yourself? Have you noticed how we tend to diminish others' mistakes and turn ours into unforgivable acts? Self-care is not just dedicating 30 minutes of the day to the routine skincare, but taking a closer look at our errors.

2.   Talk about your failures.

You don't have to share all your mistakes on social media, but finding someone you can trust to talk about your negative experiences can be liberating. Being sincere and honest about your imperfections shows that you are ready for success since there is no triumph without a considerable amount of failure.

3.   Know how to forgive to make room for the new.

Forgive those who hurt you, but especially forgive all the battles you lost and understand why it didn't work out. Mistakes are opportunities to start again, with more resources, being smarter, and with more knowledge. Do not force yourself to carry unnecessary baggage; file your errors lovingly in your self-development folder, but say goodbye to the guilt of having done wrong. The real failure is being afraid to try again.

4.   Start over as many times as you need.

Have you ever stopped to think that all great work started as drafts and every scientific formula is carried out through hundreds of trials and errors? Avoiding failure is an effective way of not dealing with your shortcomings and is a well-known self-sabotage technique. Whoever avoids failure at any cost is usually a perfectionist, and perfectionism is a convincing excuse for never starting over and remaining in the same place.

5.   Be humble.

Humble people are tolerant of each other, but above all, of themselves. We appreciate a sincere apology or when people don't get big-headed when showered with praise, or when someone accepts their failures. The truth is that the best is lost in arrogance and the worst in humility. It is not because things went wrong today that they will tomorrow. Be strong and big enough to look into the eyes of failure; be thankful for the opportunity and prepare for the next challenge. The only thing that differentiates the loser from the winner is the number of times he is willing to try.

Chapter 8

Building more prosperous relationships through communication

People do not choose to be in toxic relationships. Often, circumstances of life lead us on this path. A destructive relationship can be between parents and children, with an authoritarian boss, and even a fake friendship, but it can also be how we relate to ourselves since no other relationship requires as much honesty and commitment. As long as we are not fully aware of our greatest qualities and shortcomings, we will not know who we are and how to live to our full potential and, consequently, risk finding ourselves in toxic relationships.

Most apparent characteristics of conflicted relationships is the lack of communication, usually a consequence of traumas, lack of self-esteem, and self-limiting beliefs. However, to build healthy relationships, it is necessary, first of all, to want to be in a positive relation. But first, let's think about what defines a healthy relationship.

Whether at work or at home, a healthy relationship offers equal opportunities, respect, autonomy, attention, and freedom. The perfect relationship doesn't exist, since we are all prone to imperfections as individuals. There will be moments of discord and tension, but relationships have the potential to flourish precisely because of the ability to resolve conflicts through respect and communication. In other words, a positive relationship is one that gives us the freedom to be who we are and offers flexibility to go through moments of difficulty.

Because there is nothing more liberating than removing our masks and showing our true selves, knowing that we will not be judged or that such sincerity may one day be used against us. For this reason, the elementary premise of a successful relationship is transparency and permission to be ourselves. The more an individual makes his beliefs his own identity, the more he will distance himself from others. May our values guide us, but do not define us to the point of impeding our relationships' progress, because to relate is also to follow the flow and allow ourselves to change if necessary. There is beauty in metamorphosis, in allowing yourself to grow.

People enter and exit our lives, and relationships are not always easy. Once in a while, we are lucky: how good it is to experience the peace of a safe relationship, one permeated by kindness and empathy. But if life is a school, it is in relationships that we test our learnings. Relationships will often test us. They can take us out of our comfort zone, awaken those long-forgotten demons, and force us to face them. When that happens, finding a balance does not happen by chance: the people involved need to set the terms of the relationship if the aim is for it to succeed. This requires flexibility, commitment, and, above all, the willingness to break patterns.

Breaking patterns is vital because, in relationships, whether personal or professional, not all problems are evident. Most of them are created, developed, and multiplied in our minds through highly destructive value judgments and limits that we inflict on ourselves. It takes effort to free ourselves from our handcuffs, and the first step is to acknowledge what is hindering the success of the relationship, starting with ourselves.

The good news is that building flourishing relationships is entirely possible, but it is a process that takes time and dedication. Social networks create the false belief that ready-to-wear relationships are easy to form when, in reality, they do not exist and will never exist. Fragile relationships need to be stimulated so that, one day, they can morph into strong relationships that stand the test of time. It is only through a healthy relationship built on trust and commitment that we can experience success at work and gather the necessary confidence to realize our dreams. But for relationships to genuinely overcome all complexities of life, you need to rely on five pillars. These pillars form the necessary structure to grow together. Perfect relationships are utopic; in real life, you need the right tools and foundation to make them flourish.

The five pillars of successful relationships

1. Management of emotions

I have seen many people use impulsivity as an excuse to say what they want, when they want it, and how they want it, without a filter. More than an intrinsic characteristic, this is a practice that denotes the purest inability to manage one's emotions. Because to develop a greater understanding to build healthier relationships, first you need to know how to control your emotions.

The ability to deal with one's feelings is one of the pillars of emotional intelligence and positive communication. Without this ability, establishing a long-term and trusting relationship becomes unsustainable. In today's world of immediacy, impatience is slowly corrupting our relationships. When things don't go according to plan, the first reaction is to want to resolve everything in the heat of the moment, without giving the necessary maturation time to resolve any conflict. In the same way that non-violent communication teaches us to see the opponent with humanity, history's greatest warriors knew how to use prudence to their advantage.

By avoiding knee-jerk reactions, soldiers could make more conscious decisions and respond more appropriately to each situation, reducing the impact of their actions, which can often be damaging and cause even more discord. This is why self-knowledge is becoming more and more essential; understanding others' perspectives is, above all, necessary to look within ourselves.

2. Vulnerability

If commitment is necessary to develop positive communication, we need to show vulnerability to build successful relationships. Not just because vulnerability creates a relationship of trust, but because it establishes connections and bonds. We have always been taught to hide our weaknesses, ignoring the advantages of showing fragility. However, it is precisely by exposing our vulnerabilities that we rid ourselves of the arrogance of perfection and create bonds with others.

However, it is wrong to think that to be vulnerable is to expose yourself without boundaries. According to author Brené Brown, vulnerability is about sharing our feelings and experiences with people who have earned the right to know them.

It's not about being vulnerable to everyone, but about sharing it with those you want to build a healthy and lasting relationship. We live in the age of social media and its continuous exposure, but we have never been more afraid to show our true selves, and we have never been so attacked for doing so. But it turns out that, often, the part of us that we most want to hide is the most beautiful and noble quality we have. There is no right moment, and neither is there true perfection; the only option is surrendering to vulnerability and having a desire to build a positive relationship.

3. Empathy

There is no use in knowing how to manage our emotions and be vulnerable if we cannot put ourselves in the other person's shoes. And the most interesting aspect is that empathy can be learned; it can be stimulated and developed. After all, empathy is nothing more than putting oneself in others' position to understand their real motivations, and this realization is not innate; we were not born with that knowledge, we are building it from our lessons of past experiences.

Empathy can hurt because it requires the legitimation of other people's feelings and values, even if we disagree. Compassion is not just selfless forgiveness and generous gestures to those who are in a situation of vulnerability. In communication, empathy is understanding each person's individuality and understanding that they experience unique conditions that shape them.

Empathy requires the most unbiased listening skills: it is to understand the feelings of others, to observe without judging, and to have a presence filled with affection. If a successful relationship is one in which two or more people decide to pursue a common goal, this is only possible through empathy. It will free us from resentments and teach us to use differences as fundamental ingredients for growth.

A cake is not just a cake, but a mixture of flour, eggs, milk, and yeast. Together, they complement each other and mix with the other ingredients to form a tasty result of different qualities and origins. All ingredients add something and are essential; each has its characteristics, but none is expendable. Without any of them, the cake falls apart. The same is true of relationships: it is the mix of experiences that make people who they are, and to build a successful relationship, it is essential to accept all the ingredients without judging, just by being welcoming and offering hospitality.

4. Respect

Have you ever seen authentic and healthy relationships based on a lack of respect? No, because they don't exist. I'm talking about a real relationship, one based on partnership and kindness, not a pretend relationship on Instagram. Those are just time-wasters under the pretense of likes and comments.

For there to be respect within a relationship, it is necessary to respect ourselves, which means protecting ourselves from toxic people and hurtful relationships. I am not saying that this is easy. It is a process that requires time, commitment, and self-knowledge. First of all, we need to face the truth and accept that some people should not be part of our lives. We are the ones who teach others the way we deserve to be treated.

Something magical happens from the moment we learn to respect our limits: we are instinctively able to relate to others, openly, welcoming, but, above all, with respect. Nobody is required to please us all the time and, when we understand this, we learn to see the other as an individual full of uncertainties, fears, vulnerabilities, and difficulties the same way we struggle with our own challenges. We learn to respect their point of view and start to build effective and positive communication codes together.

Within a relationship, respect is being balanced and careful with our choice of words; sometimes, choosing to remain silent; and sometimes questioning whether what we want to say really needs to be said. Respect is more than a matter of courtesy or submission; it is gathered through all those experiences that have shaped ourselves and others; it is an evolution over time.

5. Communication

There is no shortcut: the only way to relate in a profound, sincere, and authentic way is through communication, but it only happens when we embrace the other four pillars of successful relationships. If communication were a simple exchange of information, we would not be challenged with so much confrontation, empty speeches and suffer condemned relations, suffocated by ego and power disputes.

Positive communication teaches us to listen with interest and to speak honestly. The problem is that many people listen only to answer and have the last word and not to listen to the complex myriad of narratives that is the other. The urge to be right makes us miss incredible opportunities to build bridges and real relationships, without noise and space for misinterpretation.

Do not waste time and stop fooling yourself, wanting to have a successful relationship without working on your communication skills. It is the quality of your communication that keeps two people together, whether personally or professionally. See the other, hear what they have to say, understand their vulnerabilities, and embrace their reality. Then, be assertive and honest, express your opinion without attacking the other, and without the childish need to win the debate.

Communicating is not talking, and positive communication only happens when we feel heard and understood. To be heard, listen; to be understood, understand.

Epilogue

My wish for you, dear reader

> *"In the recipe of life, I mix mistakes and successes, add joys and pains and, with a few hints of remembrance, season my existence, which without knowing whether long or brief, is certainly true, full of dreams, vulnerability and filled with intention."*

May your experiences be meaningful enough for you to turn them into learnings, but that you never lose the enthusiasm for wanting more and always going beyond. May you get lost, fall, trip, but find yourself and be willing to go through all this again, as many times as necessary. May you relate to the wisdom of an elder, but keep a child's curiosity, ready to explore the fertile environment that is the other with respect, empathy, vulnerability, and, above all, truth.

May you learn to rest when life is hard - and not to give up. May you forget once and for all the mistaken notion that the other is an opponent and embrace the greatness of being able to relate. Because, even with countless challenges, there is no substitute for trusting, holding hands, and building projects with people who are in tune with us.

May you not accept the ordinary - even if to achieve the extraordinary, you have to cross wild tides, inhospitable roads, and endless mazes. Life is abundant when we accept all its attributes, and in this school, we are all students eager for knowledge.

Be kind and have courage,

Gabriela.

PART 2

How it all began - SJ de Lagarde

'So…what actually is your job?' my brother-in-law asks. I chuckle and look down at my feet digging into the sand. I get that question a lot, as a matter of fact I have been asked this very same question for the past 20 years. By my mother.

'I advise senior leaders on communication strategies' I answer. He looks at me nonplussed, 'Is that something to do with HR?'

I shake my head.

'Marketing?'

I shake my head again and sigh. The sun is setting over the horizon, the tide is receding and the cold north 'mistral' wind flushing down the Alps is cooling the summer air.

I'm a communications adviser and in my role I oversee various communications areas such as employee communications, change and crisis communications, media relations and corporate communications. In the later part of my career I managed international media relations teams and a network of external PR agencies spanning across the globe. I advise executive committees on communications strategies, including Chief Financial Officers and Chief Executive Officers. I protect a company's reputation and build out its credibility by maintaining good relationships with members of the media. I facilitate employee engagement to have information flow from senior executives to employees, from employees back up to management and put mechanisms in place to encourage better collaboration among employees across the organisation. The stakes are often high and, as I keep reminding myself, I'm only ever as good as my last communication. In my job trust is the commodity and while a good reputation takes years to build, it also takes one ill judged communication to be destroyed.

I tried to explain this to my mother countless times, but when she introduces me to her friends she says: 'My daughter is a journalist'. When I correct her with the obligatory eye roll she says: 'Yes I know dear, but nobody knows what that comms thing is, but everyone knows what a journalist does.'

She is not wrong.

'My girlfriend is a journalist' my brother-in-law said and my ears pricked up. It turned out his girlfriend is not only a journalist but also a keen writer who was itching to write a book on the impact of positive communications. I sensed an opportunity for a collaboration, a way to combine my need to explain what my job entailed (Hey Mum) and to put down on paper some of the life changing discoveries I made over the past 20 years working on perfecting my craft.

By the time we left the beach, I had found a co-writer - Gabriela Glette, who shared my passion for communications and we had a semi hashed out outline of the book we were going to write together.

For those in the know, our pairing sounds a little out of the ordinary. See, the relationship between a public relations officer and a journalist is traditionally slightly conflicted. And generally an interesting game of give and take, subtle and not so subtle manipulation. You are frenemies - best friends discussing article topics one day and slamming down a retraction request the next. I've felt that push and pull relationship throughout my entire career. When I started off as a newbie in The City - the London financial district in 1999, I lived in fear of the smart financial journalist who in an interview asked all the questions that made my spokesperson and I quiver with nerves. I often warned my interviewees to never superficially befriend a journalist as the temptation to land an 'exclusive' is often stronger than the best of corporate friendships.

But here I was, discussing our passion for writing and communicating and bridging the gap with Gabriela Glette, my new found journalist co-author.

Chapter 9

Communication, how important can it be?

Spoiler alert very important

When I was a child, I wasn't the most popular kid in my class. Actually, let me rephrase that. I was the least popular kid in class. The awkward one who didn't look like everyone else. The odd girl with two platinum blonde plaits running down her back and who wore bright-colored hand-knitted pullovers (thanks Mum) and Birkenstocks. With socks. The fashion bunny in the 42-year-old me cringes, hard. But hey, those were the days my parents listened to Bob Dylan's Mr. Tambourine Man, dreamed of Ashram trips to India, and embraced yoga and veganism before it became a Hollywood trend.

My parents' lifestyle choices greatly impacted how I was going to be perceived by my peers. Back in the 80s, our family lived in a small village in the wild and rugged Pyrenees mountains in the South of France. My siblings and I went to a village school with less than 30 pupils. A very closed community with a distinct set of societal codes developed over centuries and saw outsiders as a threat to their traditional way of life.

I believe that beyond the fact that I was dressed like a hippy kid, my inability to integrate with my peers was not helped by the fact that I didn't speak a word of French on my first school day.

My first language is my mother's tongue: Dutch. My second language is German, which I spoke with my dad. At the age of six, I joined le Cours Preparatoire, the

French equivalent of Year 1, not knowing how to ask where the bathroom was.

The first weeks were tough. My inability to communicate was exacerbated by the fact that I looked different. I have an old class photo of that first year in school, and instantly I can see why I had such a hard time connecting with others. I'm sitting in the center of a group of French kids, all wearing their best Sunday outfits. Girls with glossy bobs, their gold communion medallions dangling from their necks and wearing checked pinafore dresses in muted colors and polished t-bar shoes. Boys are wearing pale blue shirts, v-necks, and bow ties with beige shorts and white socks. My Birkenstocks and I stand out like a sore thumb.

Quickly and unsurprisingly, I became a target for bullies.

Our primal brain, the hindbrain, and medulla urge us to seek herd approval and acceptance. In the days of cave dwellers and woolly mammoths, it was a death sentence to be rejected from the clan's safety. Without the clan's food, shelter, and protection, an individual would be exposed to the elements and predators, and their survival rate would plummet significantly. While today, most of us are no longer dependent on the clan to protect and nourish us, we have retained this innate desire to be accepted by the group throughout our evolution. Being ostracised leaves individuals feeling vulnerable.

I certainly felt exposed at first but then soon defaulted to my coping strategies: in class, I focused all my attention on the tasks my teachers gave me, ignoring the whispering and the giggles around me. As a six-year-old, I identified my weaknesses and why I wasn't going to integrate into the group. I needed to learn French and fast. I absorbed every word like a sponge. I knew that if I wanted to make friends, this was going to be the only way.

I begged my mother to buy me shiny t-bar shoes and ditch the Birkenstocks.

Necessity is the best teacher, and within a couple of months, I had mastered the basics of the French language and had toned down my wardrobe, much to the dismay of my mother, who urged me to be 'individualistic' rather than conforming. Nice try, mum, but no, I wasn't going to be swayed. I wanted to be accepted by my peers, and I was going to mirror their codes.

As I grew older, I mastered the art of 'mirroring' more and more. At first, unconsciously and then more purposefully, I started to imitate the gestures, speech patterns, and attitudes of those around me. People tend to respond well to others who resemble them. The more you look and sound like them, the more innate trust and credibility are built.

A shy kid, I spent most of my lunch breaks playing by myself, building imaginary worlds where I was in control, but I also became a silent observer. I studied my classmates' behaviors. I figured out how the class hierarchy was built.

At the top of the ladder, there was Marion, who was the top dog. A clever wealthy girl who was too posh to stay in school over lunch and would go home to eat and come back in the afternoon wearing an entirely different outfit every day. To this day, I wonder: just how big was her wardrobe? She was born confident in social situations and had just enough arrogance to be influential and gain a loyal following of less popular classmates who basked in the halo of her popularity. The weapons at her disposal were gossiping and extracting secrets from people and then cleverly use those to enslave her classmates to her cause.

There was Stephane, the class clown who had high standing because he had the entertainment factor. Making people laugh got him in trouble with his teachers on the one hand, but on the other hand, it made him popular with his peers. He was witty and sharp, with an innate ability to identify the topics and situations that would feed his comedic skits and raise his popularity even further. He also had a knack to point out his classmates' weaknesses, and that gave him authority as people were equally delighted to hear him rip a classmate to shreds with a funny but cutting anecdote and fearful of being his next target.

David, the tall, dark-haired quiet one who was the fastest runner in the school and an all-around athlete and got a pat on the shoulder by every other boy in the class. He was straightforward and fair; he had natural confidence as people around him were impressed by his physical prowess. It didn't matter that his scores were very average on the academic side; he never seemed to need to assert himself as his classmates would naturally gravitate to him and trust him to become their leader.

At the bottom of the ladder were Jerome and Nicolas. Jerome was the son of a farmer and had no interest in being in school. His grades were consistently low, and he made no effort to improve them. He was often the butt of Stephane's jokes, and the teachers gave him a hard time as he consistently remained at the bottom of the class. His physical appearance was visibly at odds with the rest of the class. His fingernails were always black, his hair disheveled, and he had a persistent whiff of manure emanating from his clothes. He would routinely arrive late in the morning, and the teacher would yell at him for falling asleep in class. It turned out that unlike his classmates, Jerome had a job. He would assist his father on the family farm and would wake up at the crack of dawn to help out cleaning out stables and feeding the cows. He would put in a day's work all before he would turn up at school.

Nicolas was a foster child. Removed from his abusive household by social services and put into foster care, he was a child from la DDASS (Direction Départementale des Affaires Sanitaires et Sociales), and with that came the stigma of being the unwanted child. It was clear from his rebellious behavior that he had experienced trauma with many unresolved psychological issues. Nicolas wasn't often given the understanding and support he needed to develop and thrive, and as a result, he withered and became angry. He often got into fights with authoritative figures such as his teachers, foster parents, and older children. His classmates equally feared and pitied him.

And then there was me. The nerd who scored the highest marks in every assignment but only had one friend, the other nerd in the class. I wanted to remain invisible and on the group's outskirts, but made mental notes following my observations to adjust my behaviors to find my place in this hierarchy.

You may recognize these characters. I, for one, have met these types over and over in my life. I married a 'David,' a tall, dark natural leader. I've met quite a few manipulating and conniving 'Marions' in my career. There's at least one funny 'Stephane' in my friends' group. We all know a 'Jerome' whose focus is divided between two worlds. And sadly, there are a few traumatized 'Nicolas' in my network who struggle to find a place in society and overcome the damage they've faced.

Eventually, I concluded that there were good and bad behaviors, there were attitudes that would make you popular, and others would get you ostracised from the group. Instinctively rather than consciously, I started to build out a set of communication codes on the back of these observations.

Here are the eight conclusions I drew:

---

1. Physical appearance matters (Jerome)

My father would say: 'Appearance is only fleeting, and it's all about personality and intelligence.' He's absolutely right, but at the same time, it goes without saying that disregarding basic hygiene rules will push people away. Take a shower, wear that deodorant, treat that acne and that athlete's foot. Perhaps note the group's dress code and tweak your style until you feel comfortable. Play with how much of yourself you can bring to the group and how much you are prepared to adapt to their codes.

2. Manipulation is an effective way to gain status (Marion)

Getting what you want from somebody else requires a degree of convincing, and manipulation is an effective way to get someone to comply with you. There are many manipulation methods, and they all need an understanding of what is essential to the other person and turn that to your advantage. But be cautious: there is a fine line between getting your way by rallying people behind your cause and taking advantage of people. Machiavellianism combined with psychopathy and narcissism are the classic characteristics of a malevolent person, so my advice would be: use manipulation methods sparingly and with no ill intent.

3. Humour opens doors (Stephane)

Humour can have various social benefits: it can defuse tense situations and strengthen social bonds between new or long-time friends. Humour is often a great way to bond with someone you might have had a tricky start with. Everyone likes a good laugh, and humor is often referred to as a Social Lubricant (I know that word sounds odd!). A sense of humor might be used as a social radar: a way to detect like-minded people. Being funny is not easy, particularly in a language that's not your mother tongue. It requires confidence, from an aptitude to see the absurdities of life to read a room, understand your audience, practice joke-telling, and make quips at the expense of yourself and situations rather than making mean spirited comments about your peers will go a long way.

4. Physical dominance increases trust (David)

Why is it that so many CEOs and Presidents are tall? Barack Obama: 1.85m, Elon Musk: 1.88m, Donald Trump: 1.9m, Larry Ellison: 1.91m, to name just a few. Several studies have shown that height and salary are positively correlated. For example, in one of the most recent studies[16] of the Fortune 500: less than 3% of CEOs were below 1.70m (5ft 7in) in height, and 90% of CEOs are of above-average height. This is an unconscious bias where the tendency is to associate the ability to lead people with physical stature. We've got evolution to blame for this unconscious prejudice. In the early stages of society, we used height as an index of power when making 'fight or flight' decisions. We associated leadership qualities with tall people because we thought they would be better able to protect us. As a consequence, tall people may have greater self-esteem and social confidence than shorter people. Some evolutionary psychologists would argue that these perceptions still endure today.

5. Gaining status by association (Marion's minions)

[16] British Medical Journal, 2017

The people we spend time with invariably end up influencing our attitudes and behaviors. They are the lens through which we view the world. We are the company we keep because people perceive us based on the actions the people closest to us display. People assume that similar individuals will spend time together. While you may be better or worse than the company you keep, it does send a signal to those who do not know you well enough to make their own judgment. If you belong to a popular group, by association, regardless of your position within the group, your status will reflect that popularity to that group's outsiders.

6. Extreme behaviors push others away (Nicolas)

We can sense quite quickly when something about a person is off. Our primal brain has a radar to warn us if someone could be potentially harmful to themselves or us. Signs of extreme behavior are often foreshadowed in speech, tone, and choice of words, as well as posture signalling the potential for outbursts or physical violence. The majority of us would probably instinctively seek to avoid confrontation with a volatile personality. Equally, those who recognize the signs and behaviors and understand their psychological meaning would be inclined to help.

7. Mirroring

To fit in, you need to identify and adopt the codes of the group. These codes can be the way you dress or speak or the activities you undertake. It takes a while to master the more subtle nuances of the codes, therefore take the time to observe what makes that group tick. I don't believe this requires a personality overhaul; I would actively discourage people from changing their personality to fit in but subtly tweak certain traits, dimming or amping them up, and tuning into the group at the right level.

8. Top Dog or Bottom Feeder?

I never made it in either category because the values in either didn't match my own. I never compromised my integrity, and my values were clear: I wanted to be honest, loyal, trustworthy, and do no harm. I didn't have the physical presence to become a sporty 'David,' and I didn't have the overt manipulation skills to become a 'Marion'. I didn't have a 'Jerome' split drive, and thankfully, I didn't have a traumatic start in life to identify as a 'Nicolas.' But I could be a 'Stephane'; entertaining others seemed a good way to gain that status. Stepping away from the bland invisible identity I had sought refuge in, I gravitated to the jokester position. I wanted to become a storyteller and spread the values I had inherited from my parents to make the world - I know it sounds cheesy - a better place.

It would take me many more years to develop my societal role, but it became clear that despite my young age, the circumstances in which I grew up would influence my whole life and the career choices I would make. With a Dutch passport, a German father, living in London, and being born and raised in France, I was a supranational citizen. I belonged nowhere but ultimately belonged everywhere. This was my definition of true freedom. I was going to develop the most efficient communications skills to integrate with all different layers of society and feel at home everywhere in the world.

Chapter 10

Diversity is what makes us stronger

When I was a kid, I was acutely aware that I was different: my clothes, my accent, my parents' penchant for patchouli and folk music. Even the things I ate - 'urgh what's that?' said my classmate as she poked her finger into my snack box. 'A tofu sandwich,' I replied. My vegetarian diet didn't sync up with my French classmates who prided themselves to have tried frog legs, tripe, and ox tongue. In those days, being different wasn't an advantage; it made you stand out but not in a good way. That Invisibility Cloak in Harry Potter (yes, I borrowed all the books from my little brother) would have come in handy at the time.

But today, the world has changed. Diversity and inclusion have made it to the top of the agenda of most corporate companies. We have gone from 'being different is not a good thing' to 'let's embrace our differences'. In the corporate world, diversity of thought is essential. For an organization to move forward, test, and implement new processes, new ways of working, and keeping high levels of creativity, you need influences from people with a different perspective. Diversity of thought is gained through having been exposed to different surroundings. Your family background, the country you grew up in, the schools you attended, and the company you keep - all these exposures will form a unique lens through which you process information and interpret them. It is of no value to have uniformity within a group unless you aim to run an unquestioned autocracy. Unchallenged 'groupthink' can lead to highly efficient societies, but they are at risk of following a leader in one direction, and what if that direction is the wrong one?

I left France at the age of 14 to move to Frankfurt am Main, Germany. By the time I left France, I had finally made a friend, and we promised to stay in touch - we didn't, but I did meet her again 20 years later. Juliette, whom I met in my 'Maternelle'[17] years, had created a successful life for herself on the island of Koh Samui, Thailand, as an entrepreneur. I celebrated my 40th under a coconut tree reminiscing with her about our school-year misadventures.

When our family arrived in Frankfurt, luggage packed up in our red 306 Peugeot; my parents enrolled my siblings and me into a bi-lingual French-German secondary school. From day one, my life changed radically. I was in another country learning new communication codes at breakneck speed: speaking a new language (Hallo, sag hast du mal 'ne Kippe?), adopting a new fashion style (forget about the French Emo/Rock N Roll carré Vichy shirts and Perfecto leather jackets, in Germany the Stüssy and Carhartt skateboard look ruled). I finally met like-minded people. There was Claudia, the daughter of an African diplomat who traveled from one country to another every two years. There was Asma, from Morocco. Blandine, who was half-French, half-German. Stephanie, from Belgium. Benjamin from The Netherlands. You get the picture. Our different backgrounds gave us unique perspectives and enriched our conversations. In group school projects, those cultural differences were particularly apparent. Our attitude to problem-solving wasn't the same, and we operated at different speeds to meet a common deadline.

---

17 Ecole Maternelle - the equivalent of Reception in the French schooling system

I observed the same phenomenon when, a few years later, I started my Master In European Business in Paris, France, and got assigned an international team to deliver a consultancy project for Arthur D. Little. We had to do market analyses and business projections for the software company, BlackBerry Limited. Our project team was as diverse as it could be: we had a near equal gender split and representation from Germany, Switzerland, France, Belgium, Italy, Spain, UK, and Mexico.

We had three weeks to present our findings back to the partners of the management consultancy firm. We quickly realized that despite the fact we all had the same objective (not making fools of ourselves in front of the jury and scoring high enough grades to pass), our approaches could not have been more different. It was hopelessly challenging for those with an inclination to be organized to reign in those who were more in the 'work desperately hard, hours before deadline' category. There were misunderstandings and fall-outs. Miscommunication led to wrong target setting, and personality differences led introverts to blend into the background and leave too much room for extroverts to take center-stage. Intellectual capital went untapped. There was ambition and confidence in one corner of the meeting room and fatalism in the opposite corner. It was fascinating and equally exhausting. I can say with absolute certainty that group projects of more than three participants were the most challenging part of the degree.

To our credit, we delivered the project by the skin of our teeth and got the Pass grade. We also accurately predicted BlackBerry's downfall, not based on its failure to expand its business offering to 'mom and pop' smartphone users, but because we ruled the design not to be sufficient 'designer'. Close enough.

Let's backtrack for a minute and look at the concept of 'diversity and inclusion' and what it means. Diversity refers to the traits and characteristics that make people unique, while inclusion relates to the behaviors and social norms that ensure people feel welcome. Human Resources professionals have long proven that recruiting from a diverse pool of candidates means a more qualified workforce. A diverse and inclusive workforce helps businesses avoid employee turnover costs. Diversity fosters a more creative and innovative workforce. Companies need to adapt to our changing nation to be competitive in the economic market. Typically areas of focus include gender, ethnicity, LGBTQ+, religion, persons with disabilities, and cross-cultural diversity.

At the start of my corporate career, Diversity and Inclusion were no more than a footnote in an HR employee handbook with little to no airtime, particularly in the financial industry. Journalists would often describe the main players of financial institutions as 'Male', 'Pale', and 'Stale.' There was not much diversity on management boards, and throughout financial organizations, the gender split was far from equal.

In my career, I had the privilege to count Dame Helena Morrissey as one of my clients. At the time, she was the CEO of a boutique asset management company, and in 2010, she founded the 30% club[18], a global campaign led by Chairs and CEOs aiming to increase gender diversity at board and senior management levels. Focusing at first on board representation in the UK, the mission has become a global endeavor with chapters active in Australia, Brazil, Canada, Chile, East Africa, Middle East, Hong Kong, Ireland, Italy, Japan, Malaysia, South Africa, Turkey, and the US.

When the campaign initially launched in the UK back in 2010, women made up just 12% of representation on

---

18 www.30percentclub.org

FTSE 100 boards. As her PR manager, I advised her on her interactions with the media and getting media attention around her efforts to increase the number of female representatives on company boards. In every interview, she would get asked, 'Why 30%? Surely you would aspire to an equal 50/50 split, why just 30%?' To which she would invariably answer: 'Research suggests that 30% represents the critical mass from which point minority groups can impact boardroom dynamics.' The 30% target was a minimum objective - it represents a floor, not a ceiling - ultimately, the aim is to reach gender balance.

Ten years later, we are still not seeing many company boards achieve that gender balance, but at least the conversation is occurring, and most companies now have stretch targets embedded into their HR programs. For example, companies listed on the stock exchange are now required to disclose their diversity and inclusion statistics in their annual reports to reassure investors that the company is leveraging diverse intellectual capital to ensure the highest return on investment.

As a young and ambitious woman, I never understood why women were so underrepresented. I always thought of companies as a micro version of our society as a whole. If the product and services we sell are targeted to a diverse set of clients, why wouldn't we have that representation inside the company? Take Mothercare plc, a British retailer founded in 1961, which specializes in products for expectant mothers and merchandise for children. It is listed on the London Stock Exchange and is a constituent of the FTSE SmallCap Index. A few years back, it boasted that it was visited by four out of every five expectant mothers in the UK, making £420m a year from its - 84 percent female - customers and claims to be 'the No1 retailer for mums-to-be and parents alike'. Yet, in 2012, there was only one woman on the board.

'Diversity is about profitability. It is not about gender, but about recognizing that companies with women at the top outperform those without, because they are more innovative' says Maxine Benson, founder of the Everywoman business network[19].

Diversity and inclusion go beyond gender equality. The US's 2020 events around police violence against a specific part of the population - black people, has quite rightly triggered a renewed focus on the racial inequalities still prevalent in our societies. Just as we need to pursue our guide to bridge the gender gap, we also need to be racially equitable.

As I continued to progress my career through international organizations, my experiences have taught me the following five pearls of wisdom:

1. Your differences are an asset

Different perspectives challenge the status quo and force us to rethink stale processes and outdated concepts. And allow us to come up with new solutions to old problems. People from all walks of life have something valuable to contribute. My father often said: 'I don't mind whether people have little or much money. If they are Catholic or Muslim. I don't care what their sexual preferences are or what color their skin is. Which political party they vote for. I don't mind any of that. And so should you'. Little ten year old me nodded eagerly, trying to make sense of what he was saying. 'But mark my words...what I do care about is whether they are smart, think for themselves, and have good values. Being honest, respectful, and tolerant, and wanting to do the right thing

---

19 Article in The Independent authored by Genevieve Roberts, 12 Feb 2012

is what counts. People who stand up tall and who contribute to making society a better place is what matters.' I remembered those words as they became my moral compass for the years to come, in a financial services environment scrutinized by the media and the general public, particularly following the 2008 financial crisis.

My uncle, at my aunt's funeral no less, laid into me. 'Out of all the industries you could've worked in, you chose to work in a bank. The epitome of greed and bottomless manipulation, I don't understand.' I think it might have been the grief talking as he had laid his wife to rest a few hours earlier, but he had a point. What did the daughter of an artist want in an industry like that? My answer surprised even me: 'You can choose to criticize the system from the outside, but you can also change it from the inside.'

2. Collaboration isn't easy

Collaborating with other people is hard. Period. Some people are easier to work with than others, but the bottom line is that working with somebody will always be a challenge. Your worldview might differ, and so might be your methodology for solving a task. Some people are more stress-proof than others; some are more dominant than others. To find balance in a team, the focus should be on solving the task at hand and identifying the core strengths of each team member. The introvert might have fantastic problem-solving skills, and the extrovert might be great at lobbying the project with external stakeholders. The GenZers might bring a whole different view on things to shake up the beliefs of a Boomer. The key is for the team leader to be able to identify those skills and give them airtime. Like a conductor and his orchestra. Allow each individual to shine with their own instrument.

3. Change takes time

Unfortunately, the bigger the organization, the longer it takes to implement change. 'But we've always done it this way' is probably the most frequent reaction when things change. Most people hate change. Our primal brain reacts to it adversely. We like to keep things as they are. Tested, safe. New ways are untested and, therefore, unsafe. The older we get, the less likely we are to seek change; a byproduct of experience is that it teaches us how to avoid surprises. We have seen scenarios unfold before and have learned from them to counter and solve them quickly when they next come around. People forget that change is good. We should be asking ourselves all the time, 'How does this work, is it still fit for purpose, how can I improve this?' Sadly only a small percentage of the population fits into this category; most think, 'I've now mastered this; how can I ensure I keep it this way?' This might explain why some diversity and inclusion efforts take a generation to move the needle.

4. Be culturally aware

Mexicans always arrive late at meetings, the Swiss are always on time, the Germans will be so organized, and the French will argue every directive. How often have we witnessed these cultural prejudices that perpetuate themselves? Most of the time, they are unfounded and somewhat arbitrary. Yet there is a deeper layer to this. We might be mildly offended by these cultural characteristics, but more often than not, the stereotypes have a foundation of truth. I can allow myself to expand on this as I have grown up across multiple cultures. My father is German, and my mother, Dutch. I was born and raised in France. I went to secondary school in Germany and university in England. I have since then worked in multi-national companies with over 30 nationalities across the teams I worked with. History and education build a culture. Traditions and communication codes spanning over decades get handed down from parents to children, and some differences permute. Being aware of the cultural backgrounds of people you interact with will help you understand the lens through which they see the world, and you can fine-tune your communications to understand and adapt to their level.

5.   Stronger Together.

Ultimately this is the only thing that matters. My husband is a keen rower with a few gold medals under his belt, and his recipe for getting in the lead in a race is not the pure strength of one or two individuals in a boat of eight. Everyone in the boat rows in the same direction, at the same speed, with the same cadence - inching closer to the finish line under the smart directive of the coxswain steering the boat. It's a commonly used analogy in the business world, and for a good reason. It is the synchronicity, the common purpose, and the value that each member of the crew adds as they play to their strength that allows them to bring their whole self to the race and win.

Chapter 11

What I learned from my burnout: #mentalhealthmatters

warning: trigger alert

There was a moment in my career where my confidence was shaken dramatically and to its very core to such extent that not only did I consider leaving the industry and the communications profession but also to end my life.

I remember the moment with extreme clarity as if etched into my brain with acid. I stood at the crossing of Camden Road and Royal College Street. Behind me was the Ladies & Gents speakeasy bar entrance, where my friends and I had enjoyed several potent cocktails on many occasions. Across the road, I could see the Curry house, a place my husband and I would often order delicious takeaway Tikka Masala and Vindaloo dishes. My friends Antje and Bruces' house was just around the corner.

It was a Monday night; I was on my way home after yet another long and emotionally draining day at work. It was dark, cold, and rainy November evening, and I held onto the collar of my parka and squeezed my handbag closer to my body to retain some heat. I looked at the pedestrian crossing, at the traffic light, and the upcoming stream of cars. It was late, way too late for a Monday night, and the familiar wave of guilt flashed through me. I was supposed to be at home cooking dinner for my girls hours ago. Yet again, I had failed as a parent and had to outsource my parental duties to the nanny at the last minute. Work was claustrophobic and crushing;

my manager had expressed concern about my performance and made it clear I had to step up. I felt stuck, not enough as a professional and not enough as a parent. The sacrifices I made on both sides of the equation weren't sufficient to satisfy both ends' expectations. I felt empty and exhausted. Panic attacks had become too frequent, and I felt like my whole life had become one interminable marathon with no end in sight.

As I waited for the traffic light to turn green, cars rushing past me splashing my high heels, something pulled at me, irresistibly, a dark force from within, whispering 'you're tired, you're a burden, you're not good at your job, and you're a bad parent and an absent wife, your friends forget about you. Your kids will be better off without you. You can't go on like this.' The voice in my head was strong and left no room for rational thinking. Robot-like I stepped towards the road. The oncoming traffic roared in my ears. I could picture the car coming closer, in slow motion, I could see the driver's eyes widening in panic, his knuckles whitening as he gripped the steering wheel tighter. I could feel the hit of the metal crushing my ribs and smashing my hips, and lifting me in the air, rolling over the bonnet like a rag doll and crashing to the floor. My face in the puddle, the red sole of my Louboutin facing upward hanging off my broken ankle, and then…lights out. I could see it so clearly; I was just one step away from deliverance.

And then an image appeared in my head, suddenly and loudly like church bells at Sunday mass, a bright glowing vision of my two gorgeous girls smiling and waving and my husband blowing me a kiss. That image was so powerful it shocked me to my core. I retracted my foot and stood still until a gentle tap on my shoulder prompted me back into reality. 'Hey lady, it's green!' I nodded and gingerly crossed the road. I made it back home okay, and gave my kids and husband a rib crushing hug. That night I told my husband, 'something has got to change; this is not how it's supposed to be.' He nodded; he had known for a while that things were out of kilter.

As I type this, I'm in disbelief; how did I get to this point? It feels like I'm writing about an entirely different person. Those close to me always describe me as a smiley, fairly stress-proof, go-getter, positive person with grit and resilience to boot. What happened to me?

Sometimes a company's culture can have a negative effect on your overall well-being. Most companies strive to have an engaged workforce and have a culture of excellence. Some implement an 'only the best work here' philosophy that flatters those who are 'chosen ones,' but an elitist culture can mask subtle bullying and backstabbing. A robust hierarchy and senior management with an 'inner circle' thinking that no outsiders can penetrate without peer validation are common. The above can lead to employees feeling under constant observation and tested to unknown criteria to see if they make the cut. Straight forward feedback isn't always given; it can be a matter of nuances in the vocabulary, timing, subtle nods, or the conversations employees are excluded from. The culture becomes toxic when speaking behind people's backs is an accepted form of communication, and employees are encouraged to share information, even confidential, about their colleagues with their managers. Coupled with an intense workload and constant competition for a promotion, or the worry to fall short of expectations can raise stress to harmful levels.

The thing with a mental breakdown is that it's a long process; it doesn't hit you on day one. It takes a slow toll on you. It builds up over time until you don't even notice how deep you have fallen down the rabbit hole. I was utterly dedicated to my job; I wanted to deliver at my highest ability to compensate for the guilt I felt as a new parent. I said yes to all the projects, mainly because I wasn't able to say no but also because I was trying to prove to myself that I was on top of things. Another project? Yes, no problem. Another crisis to manage? Yes, sure, no problem. A global event to host? Yes, absolutely, I can handle it. And so I kept adding to my remit fuelled by the fear of failure and my ego wanting me to be the best.

For months on end, I worked overtime; I was lonely and cut off from my friends and family. I was feeling so much anxiety; it was painful. My back muscles seized up from the stress and the countless hours spent in front of the computer. I knew deep down something was wrong, that I couldn't go on like this, but I didn't know how to ask for help. I didn't even know how to describe my symptoms to someone who had never suffered a panic attack. I felt like I had lost control over my life. I was a live wire, with no rubber coating to protect my core. I was exposed and raw; everything was personal; every feedback was perceived as an attack, and it chipped away at my confidence. I became restless, suffered from insomnia, and became paranoid. I caught myself unable to send an email - I kept reading it and re-reading it, looking for ways it could trigger a backlash - I was convinced I would get fired for a typo. Ironically in my line of work, a typo can indeed get you fired.

I wanted to give it all up, my job, and the industry. I didn't believe in it anymore. I felt useless with a job with no real purpose. I didn't feel anything I did made any difference to the world I lived in. While all my friends seemed to fulfill their life's purpose by setting up ethical brands that aimed to beautify the world, recycle waste and make eco-friendly products that people needed, I was still searching for my true worth.

After that night, a literal crossroads, I decided to gain back control, and following the heart-to-heart conversation with my husband, I picked up the phone first thing the next morning, and to his relief, my stubborn ass finally sought professional help.

I left my job and buried myself in home renovation works. For the first time in years, the anxiety had left my system, and all that was left was emptiness, a quiet and sunny place. For the first time, my brain was calm. All of the clutter was gone. 'It's like waking up in Joshua Tree park, in the desert, watching the sunrise, and it's quiet. So quiet' No more stress meant no more mood swings and no more restless nights wandering around the house compulsively cleaning out the kitchen cupboards. After a few months, my mind was calibrated, focused, and razor-sharp, my body had recovered, and I got back to work. In the industry. In a comms role. But this time, I was a completely different person.

Sadly I'm not alone in experiencing burnout. I have at least two close friends who came forward with very similar stories after sharing my experience. In the UK, a recent survey[20] of 2,000 working adults revealed that the average worker is most likely to experience career burnout by the age of 32. A third of respondents admit they've felt like they can't go on because of either stress or exhaustion at some point during their careers. Many (52%) say they try to do too much and don't take enough days off (39%). Nearly two in five workers (37%) feel like there's pressure to put in extra work constantly.

COVID-19 has made job burnout even worse. Many people found themselves working even more since transitioning to remote employment. Since Coronavirus restrictions began, 59% of respondents say they've started working more hours. The average remote worker has put

---

[20] Survey commissioned by The Office Group - published in the www.theguardian.co.uk 19/09/2020

in an extra 59 hours of work, the research shows. That's equal to about seven full additional days of work over the past five months. One in three respondents say that the COVID-19 lockdowns are the reason for their current feelings of exhaustion and burnout. 31% explain that they feel obligated to work more because their office is now their home. 27% are missing the social connections of traditional offices.

"With almost a third of people saying that lockdown has brought them closer to burnout, there is no question the pandemic has greatly impacted the nation's collective mental health. Companies must put defenses in place and guard against elements which might cause stress and anxiety, and looking forward; they must make robust changes to ensure employees are protected, particularly during times of uncertainty" - Dr. Sarah Vohra, consultant psychiatrist.

For many years, Mental Health had not been on the radar for many organizations until it became apparent that 1 in 4 suffers from a psychological condition that can significantly impede their ability to work. Employers realized that ignoring their duty of care towards employees on the mental health side would cost them in the long-term. Over the past ten years, the narrative has changed from 'Why should we improve our organization's mental health to 'How can we improve the mental health of our organization.'[21]

I increasingly became aware of our minds' impact on our ability to function at work. I co-founded a companywide Mental Health Awareness Employee Resource Group with two like-minded colleagues. Our aim was three-fold: creating openness around mental health, improving mental health literacy, and taking

---

[21] Source: www.citymha.org.uk

practical steps to improve the mental health of our colleagues. As part of this initiative, I completed a Mental Health First Aider course[22]. While the training was intense, it taught me more than just naming the different conditions and recognizing the symptoms. It taught me to observe and listen, become a trusted advisor, and sign-post sufferers to the relevant professionals. I understood the need for us to look out for the mental condition of the people we interact with and look after our own. It is essential that leaders, managers, and colleagues take the time to find out what is happening to a person's whole life, rather than just within working hours. Only then will we be able to support people appropriately and enable them to fulfill their full potential.

Going into my new role, with more responsibility and managerial duties than ever before, my concerned mother asked me, 'Are you sure, remember what happened last time?' How could I forget? The memory was etched in my brain as if with acid. 'I've learned from this experience, it won't happen again,' I answered… and here are the five things I promised my mother:

1. Know your limits

Stress is meant to be a 'fight or flight' mechanism designed to be used sparingly and with laser-like intent. In cavemen days, when faced with a saber-tooth tiger, your surge of adrenaline would shut off the rational brain - the NeoCortex - and activate the so-called Lizard brain - the Cerebellum - which is responsible for our instincts and gives you the strength to either fight the predator or run as fast as you can to safety. Stress can, therefore, be useful if experienced in bursts. However, nobody is immune to

---

[22] www.MHFAengland.org

long-term stress, and eventually, your mind and body will reach a limit. Some people can handle a stressful environment for longer than others, but ultimately, symptoms tend to catch up with everyone, and people see physical and emotional manifestations of the stress such as back pain, mood swings, panic attacks, or sometimes heart conditions and even some types of cancer. During the lockdown, research showed that we sustain long-term damage to our psyche beyond six months of continuous stress. Therefore know your limit, and stop to recalibrate before you reach your tipping point.

2. Learn how to say no and to delegate

A rookie managerial mistake is to fear to let go of responsibilities. But the simple truth is you won't be able to do it all, and if you keep saying yes to each task, the overall quality of your work may suffer. Saying no strategically is essential to safeguard your workload and your sanity. If you are managing others, delegation comes with trust and good communication; you need to clearly articulate what you want your delegate to deliver to see the results you expect. And then you need to trust them. Their way of working may differ from yours. Their lens onto the world is different from yours, and you will need to find the right balance between delivering precisely to your vision and a slightly evolved version of it. And in fact, delegating also raises your status, i.e., giving others a platform to shine ultimately reflects well on you as their sponsor or mentor.

3. Your mental state dictates how you communicate with others
   (with your manager, stakeholders, and employees)

If you feel stressed and under pressure, you project that inner feeling to the people around you, and people react to you accordingly. The more paranoid you get to make a mistake, the more likely you will be controlling and overpowering others. The more insecure you become, the more likely it is for others to second guess you. The more overwhelmed you are, the more likely people will underestimate your abilities. The angrier you are, the more likely people will respond in anger. Looking after your mental state and aspiring to be calm and collected will positively impact the people around you. You need to feel secure in yourself to be able to convey your message efficiently to others. Positive communication starts with you.

4. Seek professional help when needed

Be aware of your mental state. If you experience long periods of unhappiness and increased irritability, and other symptoms of burnout or depression such as insomnia, heart palpitations, or panic attacks, please seek help. Speak to a trusted family member, a mental health first aider, HR, or your GP and ask to be referred to a mental health specialist such as a psychotherapist, psychologist, or, if needed, a psychiatrist. There are many forms of therapies, including talking therapies or medication, and a mental health professional can guide you to the most effective one for you.

5. Mental Health matters, and so does self-care

As a newly minted mother with career ambition, I often found myself spread way too thinly. Wanting it all but spending so much energy on spinning all the plates that eventually, it all came crashing down. Have you noticed that when they show you the emergency procedures film in airplanes, they always advise you first to put the oxygen on your face and then look after your child? I always had found that odd, indeed you would first look after your child and then yourself. Here's the thing: if you run out of oxygen, you can't save your child, which is true more generally. If you don't look after yourself, you won't be able to look after those around you because you will have run out of oxygen.

You are not alone. Even though, at times, it feels like you are the only one suffering, you would be surprised as to how many people experience the same symptoms. I found out that when I told others about my experience with panic attacks, people shared their insecurities and anxieties with me in return. A Gallup study in 2019 of nearly 7,500 full-time employees found that 23% reported feeling burnt out sometimes. No-one is immune from burnout. It can hit the overworked and undervalued high-achieving executive, the nurse or clergy who provide care to others around the clock, or the everyday employee trying to get to the top. It's a topic to be aware of and talk openly about so you know the signs and prevent it. [23]

23 Bryan Robinson Ph.D in Forbes Jun. 2 2019

Chapter 12

How to build trust

Even if I'm employed by the company I work for, I always take a consultant's view. I try to come in with an outsider point of view, and having had the experience of being an outsider growing up; I'm entirely comfortable in that role. Most of my clients are senior executives of international companies with status and seven-figure salaries. Most of them have razor-sharp intellect, an ego the size of a small country, steel elbows, and a very low tolerance for mistakes. Working with this particular demography requires an adequate level of confidence in your capabilities.

Unfortunately, while I had accumulated quite the experience, I was still plagued with impostor syndrome, a psychological pattern in which you doubt your accomplishments or talents. I was constantly tormented by a persistent internalized fear of being exposed as a fraud. 'Somebody is going to find out that I know nothing about this,' that confidence destroying thought reared its ugly head ever so often. Mostly after a perceived failure or a telling off from a manager, justified or not.

It takes much self-confidence to speak up and advise a senior executive ranking at least two levels up from your position. It's all well and good when you can tell them that they are doing a great job, but sometimes you have to suggest doing things differently - reshoot a video, change how they present, or amend their talking points in an interview. It's not easy when your interlocutor is your boss' boss' boss, and to be successful, I had to understand what made this hierarchy so intimidating and find my place in it, a place that would allow me to keep my integrity and do my job without the fear of failing.

I don't believe in sycophantic behaviors, as flattery is fleeting and isn't a catalyst for building dependable authentic relationships. I believe in honesty and transparency. Hierarchy is a complex social construct based on a system in which we are ranked according to relative status or authority. The keyword being 'relative.' If you say something is relative, you mean that it needs to be considered and judged in relation to other things. In essence, there is a perceived higher authority and a perceived lesser authority that isn't worth much when taken out of context. Imagine the Queen of the United Kingdom getting abducted by aliens. Would they see her for what she is - a strong elderly woman or treat her with the same pomp as we would, curtseying and formally addressing her 'Your Majesty' and subsequently 'Ma'am' pronounced with a short 'a' like in 'jam'?

Hierarchy provides structure and categorizes people according to specific criteria, a natural development in our societies, but the financial industry in which I grew up, more often than not, seems to be based on superficial material value. How much the individual earns, their bonus, the number of people who report to them, their car's size, or the postcode of their home(s); their influence on a larger number of individuals. These criteria seem to matter more than the wisdom and experience acquired over time and their expertise in their field. A hierarchy benefits those at the top of the pyramid and rarely those at the bottom. I've seen whip-smart junior team members wither away, having to photocopy and bind reports for years to 'pay their dues.' I know, as I was one of them.

I used to coordinate investor roadshows when I started in investment banking in one of the top five firms in this space, and I was told 'to start at the bottom' to 'work my way up.' So I bound endless copies of roadshow presentations, my master's degree in my pocket, and my four languages unused, until I had enough and resigned. But I learned a lot, nevertheless; the main thing being that I didn't want to pursue a career in investment banking.

I also learned another valuable life lesson, taught to me by the CEO of a well-known German airline, on a day I wished the ground I stood on would swallow me up.

I was at a luxury hotel in Frankfurt am Main, Germany, desperately trying to fire up my laptop to play the presentation the CEO was supposed to speak to, in front of an audience of high profile investors. The room was filling up with men in sharp dark suits and one stern looking woman with a tightly knotted chignon and diamonds dangling from her ears. I was getting increasingly sweaty under my hairline as whatever I did, I couldn't find the file I had saved an hour earlier in the office. I started to panic, knowing full well that time was of the essence, and I was about to let this man down as well as my boss and the company. I was probably going to lose my job over this technical error, at least that's what my brain, foggy with fear, concluded.

The impostor syndrome woke up and whispered, 'You fool, you don't even know what you're doing.' And then the CEO towered over me. 'Having a little trouble?' He asked, cool as a cucumber. My clammy hands were shaking. My instinct was to lie, to run a mile, to blame it on someone else, but all I could muster was: 'I'm sorry, I tested it twice back at the office, and it worked. I won't have time to run back to upload it again, and we might have to delay the start of the presentation. I'm sorry. It's my fault; I should've tested it with an IT colleague and should've been here earlier.'

The CEO nodded and reached into his pocket: 'and that's why I always carry a copy of the presentation on an extra device,' he plopped the CD (yes, it's that long ago...) into the laptop, and sure enough, the presentation sprung to life. As he walked on stage, he turned to me and winked, 'Remember this: technology will always let you down, always have a backup plan.' One of the most valuable lessons I've learned, would you believe it. I now always carry multiple devices, extra batteries, printouts of my notes, and always ask myself - what if the tech lets me down, what's my plan B?'.

I believe to this day that my honesty and good intent struck a chord with this man, and instead of ripping me to shreds, he saw that I was genuinely pained and that I shouldered the responsibility for this snafu[24]—that, and probably the look of sheer terror on my face.

At the end of the day, the people in senior positions are also just people with fears and aspirations. Their experiences are at a different level, but their basic emotional needs are the same. Early on in my career, I remember how I was terrified of speaking publicly, and my mentor said: 'Just picture them naked; we all look the same without clothes on.' Though great advice in theory, it didn't help me much getting over my fear of public speaking as now not only was I nervous, I now also was distracted, picturing saggy genitalia squished on office chairs.

At work, a more senior person than you may influence your performance and career progression, and that may feel intimidating, but they also know that they rely on their advisers to steer them to make the right decisions in their senior position. Naive as I was, I thought you could only climb the corporate ladder and become more senior once you had absorbed all the knowledge from everyone in your team. So, a CEO could only become

---

24 SNAFU: informal - a confused or chaotic state, a mess. Military slang: Situation Normal, All Fucked Up

CEO once he became an expert in every discipline in his company. It turns out that's not how it works; it's a little bit more complicated and straightforward at the same time. Of course, knowledge and expertise are the main drivers for the corporate ladder ascent, but not exclusively. Political and networking skills, knowing how to influence and move people out of the way when they work against you. All that counts.

And yes, chance too.

So far, in my career, honesty and transparency have served me well. Now, of course, both those come with a healthy dose of emotional intelligence, which allows you to read the personality you interact with and modulate your response. I have made a few costly mistakes along the way, which I could kick myself for in hindsight, but they were also great learnings. I decided that I had enough experience in my field to be considered an expert, and that gave me the confidence to provide advice, even to those who were ten years my senior and earned my salary multiple times over.

Strangely, I have never been too easily impressed by status and only lost my cool a couple of times. Most of my career I've spent working with some heavyweight personalities, but a few stuck.

I once made Jean-Pierre Raffarin, the former Prime Minister of France, laugh as I prepared him for a conference panel. I can't remember what I said, probably something mildly offensive about Brexit, but his usually stern face scrunched up into a smile.

I once arranged a press briefing with Sir Roger Carr, the chairman of Centrica Plc, the largest British multinational energy, and services company that supplies us with electricity and gas listed on the London Stock Exchange and returning billions in revenue. He was charming, polite, and even, despite all his responsibility, a little reserved. I was surprised when he asked me how I thought the interview went and what he could have done better. I didn't know he would be interested in my views, but I gave him my honest advice, and he thanked me for it. I remember being impressed by his humbleness.

I once booked Dame Ruby Wax, a well-known British-American author, actress, and comedian, for a private corporate event on her How to be Human tour. On camera, she is sharp and witty. Full of confidence and energy. I would say she is intimidating. However, when I welcomed her to our venue, she wasn't the sharp-tongued woman I expected her to be. She was kind and, dare I say it - nervous. Before going on stage, I was in the wings with her, the clock was ticking, and I counted down the minutes to the moment I would lead her into the auditorium. Suddenly she shrunk into the seat next to me, looking slightly panicked. 'How is my makeup looking? Do you have lipstick?' She asked. I laughed, 'I sure do.' Luckily, I had one in my makeup bag in one of those colors that matches everyone's complexion.

She put it on and asked me, 'Do I look like someone who knows their stuff?' I nodded and then realized what was happening. The Impostor Syndrome voice was whispering in her head. I could feel time was running out. 'I'm not sure I can do this,' she whispered. I thought about the 200 people sitting in the audience waiting for her appearance, I thought of the CEO waiting to introduce her, and I thought of my reputation. I squeezed her arm, 'Hey, don't listen to that voice, you are awesome; all the millions of times you went on TV and aced it, this is no different. You'll be great, and I'll sit in the front row; just talk to me if you feel a bit wobbly' She took a deep breath, got up, and walked into the room. She was brilliant and didn't look at me once during her 1-hour performance. As I walked her back to her car, I told her, 'That was awesome!' 'So were you - thank you,' she said and hugged me. Celebrities, huh? They're just like us.

I once went to see a play in a tiny London theatre featuring a young Max Irons, the son of acclaimed British actor Jeremy Irons. The play was Farragut North, which later became the movie "The Ides of March," it's an extraordinary journey into the underworld of politics from Beau Willimon, head writer of the hit US version of House of Cards. Max Irons was brilliant in Stephen Bellamy's role, a bright young man who is press secretary to a candidate for the Democratic Party's presidential nomination. After the play, my friend and I went for a cheeky cigarette outside the venue. I was scrambling through my handbag for a lighter when my friend elbowed me: 'Look, it's him, over there!' He was having a fag and a laugh with his crew. I walked over and asked for a lighter. Feeling emboldened, I quipped, 'I have to say, amazing performance' he smiled, and I continued talking 'shame about that one time you fluffed your lines' his face fell, and I realized that split second that he was hurt. I laughed. 'Dude, I'm pulling your leg. You were flawless through that massive monologue'. He exhaled. 'Oh gosh, thanks, you had me worried.' He probably thought that wasn't funny at all. His reaction highlighted that I had forgotten he was a person and probably was nervous and worried about failing.

I didn't think I would ever be the fainting fan type, nor that I would be impressed by status. Until the day I met the Queen of the United Kingdom. At the time, I worked at a British FTSE100 company, and when we moved into its newly built offices, we got word that no less than Queen Elizabeth II would be unveiling the plaque for the inauguration. Understandably there was an air of excitement in the weeks and days before her arrival as we prepared for what was to become the most meticulously orchestrated event I'd ever been part of. There were grandstands erected in the entrance hall. The ceremony was being broadcast live to all of our offices across over 25 countries. We had conference rooms and auditoriums converted into screening rooms. We had employees stationed across the building to greet the monarch at every step throughout her one hour visit of the building. I was part of the organizing committee, so I knew I would get to see her up close. I, however, did not realize how close that ended up being. My colleague pulled me to one side and whispered that not only would I meet her, but I would also actually speak to her. I was surprised but took it in my stride. Yes, fine, no problem. I was to give her a 2-minute explanation of my role and the Mental Health Employee Resource Group I had co-founded.

I smiled at all those around me, fussing and buzzing. The excitement in the air was palpable. Yet, I remained eerily calm. It must be because I'm not necessarily a royalist; also, I'm not English, I thought to myself. In any case, it was an advantage at this point as I could see my colleagues turning a whiter shade of pale as the Queen's entourage approached us to signal her imminent arrival. There were minders in full military uniform. Our company's chairman, CEO, and other senior members of the management committee were present. And there she was. Wearing a hat and coat in the same teal color, she wore block heels and held a small handbag. She looked exactly like the photos you'd see of her. As she came closer, I frantically tried to remember the instructions the palace had given us: greet her with 'Her Majesty,' curtsey, you may touch her gloved hand if she presents it to you but talk for no longer than 2 minutes. I tried to remember what I was meant to say. Somehow the only thought I had in my head was Brexit, and why hadn't she stepped in to stop it from happening. Of course, I couldn't ask her that, as the monarch, she has to remain politically impartial!

And then there she was, listening to my colleague on my right. I was next in line. I could feel all my blood rush to my head, and I quivered in my high heels. A choice of footwear I regretted instantly as she stood before me, half my size. She may be of diminutive stature, but the aura around her was compelling. I thought my heart was going to jump out of my throat. She's just a grandma; I tried to reassure myself… a grandma to Prince William and Prince Harry! It was all over in 2 minutes. I manage to deliver my lines. She smiled and said, 'Mental health? Well done for making that a priority; it is essential indeed. Charles will be pleased to hear this.' I was blown away. She had listened to what I'd said and reacted to it. She was 94 years old and had spoken to dozens of people in the last 30mins and yet she was present and listened. I was deeply impressed. The place where her gloved hand had touched mine was glowing.

In most professions, trust is the currency. People accept your advice because you have enough experience and expertise to reassure them you know what you're doing. Over the years, I have perfected my craft and have learned to find my place in large corporations' hierarchies, and the key to it is to be respectful of senior statuses but not be intimidated by them.

Here are the seven pieces of advice I would give my younger self.

1. Trust yourself first

Trust can't be bought, it must be earned, and before you can gain someone else's trust, you must have confidence in your abilities. Trust yourself first, and the rest will follow. Become a real expert in your field, increase your confidence, and people will want to seek your advice and opinions.

2. Don't compromise on your values

You don't need to become a sycophant. Be the best you can be, be straightforward, be honest, be transparent. The majority of people will react positively to authenticity. Trust is defined as to have confidence, faith, or hope in someone. It is earned by being authentic, delivering against your promises, and doing so consistently. You only get to betray one's trust a couple of times before it is eroded and, ultimately, lost.

3. Don't erode your trust capital

Trust takes a long time to build, but it can be eroded rapidly through mistakes that discredit the trust capital you've spent time and effort to build. You might get away with one or two errors, depending on their severity, but beyond that, it won't be easy to recover. Having a policy of 'no surprises' will help front possible adverse outcomes. Warn your stakeholders if there's negative news on the horizon, share the actions you have taken to minimize the fallout, and if a genuine mistake happened, speak up in earnest, apologize, and move on. Your candor and authenticity will be appreciated.

4. Don't be impressed by the wrong things

It's easy to succumb to the flair of the moment of ostentatious displays of wealth (and lack of taste mostly) perpetuated by Netflix series such as Selling Sunset, The Kardashians, The housewives of [insert city name] and visible on influencers' curated-to-perfection Instagram accounts. But these superficial perceived hierarchical constructs are masking the essential things that matter in life. Be more impressed by someone's knowledge, vulnerability, sense of humor, and humbleness, which to my mind are way more impactful and lasting than the ability to sport the latest Gucci handbag or drive the newest Landrover Defender. Now don't get me wrong, you can have both style and substance, but if I were made to choose, I'd go for substance and be impressed by that.

5. Don't forget that senior individuals are people

Sorry I know that does sound like a cliché; I have found that time and time again, although locked in ivory towers, the people in charge are people governed by the same needs as everyone else. This includes emotional characteristics such as self-doubt, need for confirmation, fear of rejection, and stress. They might experience it on different levels, but they will have the same emotional characteristic as you and me unless a psychopath (and they do exist in the corporate world).

6. Give before asking

Here's an important lesson that I wish I had come up with by myself, but my husband reminded me of this one. Giving before asking is a great way to build trust. In dark psychology[25], the practice of reciprocity is used as an effective way to build ties with someone to manipulate them. Reciprocity is the practice of exchanging things with others for mutual benefit, especially privileges granted by one person to another. I don't support Dark Psychology practices and would instead look at it from the perspective

---

[25] While Psychology is the study of human behaviour and is central to our thoughts, actions and interactions, the term Dark Psychology is the phenomenon by which people use tactics of motivation, persuasion, manipulation and coercion to get what they want.

of building trust before asking something of your stakeholder. As in, don't ask for a promotion if you haven't yet proven your worth first.

7. Don't wear 12cm high heels when you meet the Queen of the United Kingdom

This is a simple rule, and it goes back to my initial thoughts in chapter 1: the mirroring exercise. To increase trust, you mirror your interlocutor. Not necessarily just in the fashion stakes but also the attitude, language, both verbal and physical. Find the similarities that link you to the person you seek to build a trusted relationship with. Familiarity and recognition have an instant effect of giving your interlocutor a sense of security and a feeling of 'being on the same page.' In my case, I didn't want to tower over Her Majesty and felt that in hindsight, I should have probably worn flat shoes instead of the 12 cm pumps.

Chapter 13

How to stay calm in a crisis

Have you ever had that sliding door feeling where you've been in a situation that you know could have propelled your life in a completely different direction? I had one of these moments when I first moved to London back in the 00s. Fresh out of university with a master's in Foreign Applied Languages in my luggage, I was looking for a job. In those days, even though the internet existed and you could search for jobs online, you still had job ads in the local newspapers.

I remember flipping through the pages rather listlessly; many ads were for cleaning personal, estate agents, glamour models, and call center operators. But one ad stood out from the rest 'What are you waiting for? A change? Something new and different? A challenge, perhaps?', it did mention something about being multilingual and multicultural and that a sense of adventure was a necessity. I was intrigued enough to ignore the fact that it didn't mention any company name and that the job description in itself was very vague. There was a number to call and a nondescript email address. I sent in my CV, and sure enough, a couple of days later, I was asked to meet for an interview.

I was given a time and a location. The address was in central London, adjacent to Charing Cross train station. I checked the address twice as I stood in front of a rather run-down looking greasy spoon. Inside the cafe, it smelled of fried eggs and bacon. I looked around the place, and aside from the overweight owner behind the counter, there was only one other person in the cafe. The man was middle-aged and wore a three-piece tweed suit with a starched white shirt. Just as I thought I had the wrong place and ready to turn on my heel, he raised his hand and beckoned me over.

'It's lovely to meet you, Sarah, please have a seat,' he spoke in a posh-clipped British accent, and with his floppy hair, he reminded me of a character Colin Firth would play. I sat down and got my CV out, vaguely rattled that he knew my name even before I had introduced myself but ready to answer the man's questions. It turned out he asked me lots of them. Where I was from, my work experience, why I had chosen to study business, how long I had spent in the UK, what I thought of the country and its government, what type of passport I had. He sipped his tea, his blue stare not betraying any emotions. I started to wonder what the hell I had gotten myself into when he asked me about my relationship with my family, whether I was close to them, and how often I would visit them and how I would feel not seeing them for long periods. I thought the questioning was getting a little odd. Mostly since every time I enquired what the job entailed, he elegantly deflected from responding. He was very polite, which gave the false impression that he was friendly, but I could sense that he was as hard as nails behind the tweed and the pleasantries. He took the last sip from his teacup, wiped his chin with a clean white handkerchief, and leaned back on the mustard-colored sofa.

'I'm awfully sorry, but I don't think your profile fits the position we are looking to fill but thank you ever so much for taking the time to speak with me.' He leaned forward and folded his hands on the table.' You'll do very well in your career. Goodbye.'

I was stunned by the abrupt response, and I mumbled something to the effect of goodbye and backtracked out of the cafe. On my way home and ever since I wondered what that had been all about. Who was that man, and what was the job I applied for and didn't get?

So obviously, I let my imagination run wild and was convinced that it had been a recruitment interview for MI5 or MI6[26] secret intelligence service if only that didn't sound too much like a Guy Ritchie movie scenario.

I eventually found a job as a special agent, not in the secret services, but at UPS, the American international package delivery and supply chain management company. Instead of the glitz and glamour of spying, I was stewarding special delivery packages across the globe as a special agent. Before the days of Amazon and its next day deliveries, we were a pilot project for international overnight emergency delivery services. I was thrilled; it was a lively and exciting job. Our team spoke over 17 languages and worked around the clock, seven days a week. We were the first team to adopt an agile mindset, work night shifts and were early adopters of remote working practices.

We were given Dell laptops and Nokia 5110 mobile phones as big as bricks. Our job was to coordinate the international shipping of big spare parts for power plant turbines, publishing printers, and hospital generators from some giant desert warehouse in Texas to wherever in the world the spare part was needed. We were end-to-end agents, which meant we were on call 24/7, and when the engineer would place the emergency call through to us, we would spring into action and had less than five minutes to log in, locate the part in the warehouse, and place the call to reserve it.

---

[26] MI5 (Military Intelligence) protects the UK against threats to national security such as terrorism, espionage and sabotage, the activities of agents of foreign powers, and form actions intended to overthrow or undermine parliamentary democracy by political, industrial or violent means. MI6 is its foreign intelligence equivalent.

And while the warehouse technicians would get the spare part ready to be loaded, we would locate appropriate transport, prepare the travel documents and the customs paperwork. The clock was always ticking; time was of the essence. We knew that sometimes hundreds of thousands of dollars were at stake; even, at times, lives; and that we were running against the clock. We would accompany the driver over the phone and guide him through express customs and loading bays until he handed the part over to the handler, who would then load it into the overnight freight plane. Sometimes, if we missed the cut off time for freight planes, we would think creatively and book a commercial ticket. One specific spare part, the size of a coffin, that in itself was worth so much that we would book a commercial plane seat for it. We would also buy the handler a ticket to sit next to it until it reached its destination. We'd track the parcel either live over the phone or monitor its scanning checkpoints to track its progress across the world's map. It was exhilarating. Once the plane took off, we had a few hours until it reached its destination airport, and we had to be vigilant to ensure we had the appropriate paperwork ready at the other end and the final part of the journey tightly organized. We would be in charge until the spare part was delivered at its destination, a hospital, a factory, or a newspaper printer, and our mission was only complete when the delivery was signed off and in the safe hands of the engineer. Most of the time, we were able to deliver in less than 24 hours.

Our team of special agents was small, we were about 20-25 people, but we had a team leader, an ex-army general, who ran the operating model with precision and instilled a great sense of camaraderie among the team. There was no 'I' in his team, and we were seamlessly working together and handing over projects and responsibilities as we worked our shifts. It was a culture of collaboration.

There were some evident parallels between the military and the way we worked. Not only did I have to learn all the Airport codes - the IATA[27] 3-letter location identifiers such as LAX for Los Angeles, FRA for Frankfurt, VKO for Moscow. I also had to memorize the military phonetic alphabet, which uses 26 code[28] words to represent each letter of the alphabet— A for Alpha, B for Bravo, C for Charlie, etc. Since we worked with people across various countries speaking English as their second or third language with varying accents, it was essential to use the same phonetic alphabet to detail error-free spelling and reduce pronunciation discrepancies during phone conversations. You may be familiar with the shortcode used in movies when soldiers communicate with each other using sayings such as 'Oscar-Mike' which is a shortcode for 'On the Move' or slang like 'Bravo Zulu,' a naval signal meaning 'Well Done' or 'Tango Mike' for 'Thanks Much' and even the slightly more sinister 'Tango Uniform' - 'Toes up' used to report a death.

On a larger scale, military communications have precision and clarity that inspired me throughout my entire career. Communication during military operations can be the difference between losing a comrade or bringing everyone home. Efficient communication allows you to direct your troops and can win or lose wars. The ability to receive and use precise and timely information is of critical importance on the battlefield. It can often spell the difference between victory or defeat.

---

[27] International Air Transport Association

[28] www.militarybenefits.info

The precision is reflected in an ability to remain calm under intense pressure, to be able to go into protocol mode instantly and to follow the process outlined without letting emotions such as nerves or panic interfere. Once in protocol mode, it is all about making the right decisions without hesitations. Timing is crucial when dealing with a crisis scenario, and as a communications professional, you are in the eye of the storm, on the front line, and in charge of relaying information to various stakeholders in a precise and transparent manner. Needless to say that it isn't easy, but experience steadies the hand and having a clear mapped out framework to respond to those 'what if...' situations is key to success.

In the modern world, most nations attempt to minimize the risk of war caused by miscommunication or inadequate communication. In the UK, the Royal Corps of Signals was one of the British army's combat support arms responsible for military communications, particularly during the world wars. Signals units were among the first to spring into action providing the battlefield communications and information systems essential to all operations. Their motto, Swift and Sure, reflected the need for timely and precise communications.

You may be familiar with MI5 and MI6, but far less known is MI7: a now-defunct branch of the British War Office's Directorate of Military Intelligence with responsibilities for press liaison, censorship, and propaganda during the first and second world war. MI7 was designed for psychological warfare and supported intelligence gathering and communication between adversaries, and thus sometimes prevented conflicts, sometimes by controlling the public reporting of battles, amplifying successes and minimizing defeats, and sometimes by influencing adversaries into surrender. All this without weapons, but using words instead - a reminder that the written word matters much and misinterpretations can be costly.

Corporate communicators and media relations experts often deal with unexpected, unplanned situations, ranging from sudden key person departures, regulatory fines, product failures, activist shareholders, mergers and acquisitions which impacts not just the business in itself (and its employees, shareholders, and clients) but also the industry overall. Speed and clarity are critical, mainly when the situation is confusing and uncertain.

Building a tightly-knit team, where all members are specialists in their areas of expertise, with a flat hierarchy under strong leadership and an inbuilt succession planning will serve leaders well in times of crisis. This became particularly relevant when the global pandemic hit, and most companies needed to move their workforce to work from home in less than two weeks. Managers had to ensure that with the possibility of team members contracting the virus, they had a robust contingency succession plan. They increased the frequency of their virtual team meetings to allow their employees to interact with each other and, crucially, ask the questions they needed answering and delegating tasks to team members to even workloads. The familiarity and distinct role assignments prove their worth when the team finds themselves in a crisis. Clear instructions are given and executed as per standard protocols, and the team remains cool-headed throughout the situation.

In general, we naturally are risk-averse and take comfort in clearly established routines. We seek to avoid unplanned change and generally are flustered when an event derails our set up. However, the uncomfortable reality is that change is the only constant these days, and success and failure are determined by our ability to adapt quickly to that changing environment. While, by definition, we cannot predict an unexpected change, we can adopt a mindset that is agile enough to adapt to any given situation.

Here are some tips to keep in mind when the proverbial hits the fan and you want to remain cool-headed in a crisis.

1. Be prepared

Preparation is everything, and scenario planning is critical. You wouldn't go into battle without a plan, and hence you shouldn't face a crisis without some form of preparation. Think of the worst that can happen, and then plan specifically to respond to that scenario. Always have a plan B, and even a plan C in case plan A doesn't work out. Devise a written process and rehearse the steps beforehand. If it involves a team, get briefing sessions in place, and assign specific responsibilities to each team member.

2. Breaking News - what now?

Remember that when the crisis first breaks, you will be overcome with a sense of panic. The key thing is to shake off the emotions as quickly as possible, take a deep breath, switch over to crisis mode, and follow protocol. Tick off the steps as you go through them. Once you are focused and steady, assess the situation, think back to the plan and adapt to the right scenario. Make your decisions quick and assertive, don't second-guess yourself, remember: you rehearsed for this! I do this for a living, but this crisis mode thinking does come in handy at a personal level too. I once took a phone call late in the evening with some sad news, a relative had had a fatal accident, and I had to alert various family members. I had been very close to the person who died, and for a split second, I felt utterly winded by the news. But sure enough, my crisis mode thinking took over and eclipsed my emotions to leave me sufficiently clear-headed to map out the next steps I had to take, i.e., phoning my relatives and providing emotional support for them. In psychology, this disassociation of emotions is called compartmentalization. It is a defense mechanism where you suppress your thoughts and feelings. It's not always done consciously, and you need to be aware that while emotions aren't harmful in themselves, issues arise when these unhandled emotions affect your focus, motivation, and productivity.

3.   Be efficient in your communications

It is not a coincidence that much military jargon has crossed over in the corporate world, and in communications, we are often guilty of using these expressions. Most of the time, it is to sound cool and psyche ourselves up to take out the fear of the event. However, it serves a real purpose to shortcode: saving time and conserving confidentiality. For example, we use code names for confidential projects such as 'Project H2O; expressions such as 'ETA' - Estimated Time of Arrival or 'A-Day' - Announcement Day. You often hear us shout down the line:' Fire in the hole' - the warning that an explosive detonation in a confined space is imminent. It originated from miners and soldiers, who needed to warn their fellows that a charge had been set. This expression is used in our context when a change communication plan is launched and a press release distributed, and a breaking news story is published. In written communications, less is more. Be precise in your instructions; be clear in your key messages and calls to action. When determining timeframes, we use the military clock, a 24-hour clock, beginning at midnight (0000 hours).

Common Corporate Vocabulary

Some of the more common expressions that incorporate jargon are very cheesy, such as the unbearable 'Blue sky thinking,' which refers to brainstorming with no limits. With this approach to idea generation, ideas don't need to be grounded in reality. Instead, Blue Sky thinking sessions are open to all creative ideas regardless of practical constraints.

I had a manager who would always use the expression: 'Tilting at windmills', which means engaging in conflict with an imagined opponent - attacking imaginary enemies - originating from Miguel de Cervantes' early 17th-century novel Don Quixote.

What about 'thinking outside the box'? An overused metaphor that means to think differently, unconventionally, or from a new perspective.

And the awful sounding 'low hanging fruits': a commonly used metaphor for doing the simplest or easiest work first or for a quick fix that produces ripe, delectable results.

We often remove 'roadblocks' or 'bottlenecks' - obstacles to complete our projects. We 'ring-fence' our budgets and 'safeguard' our teams. We 'deflect' our answers and 'deploy' tactics. Our communications strategies are 'reactive' or 'proactive.'

Here are some examples of commonly used military-inspired vocabulary:

Situations are often color-coded: green, amber, and red. If the late-night message on your phone flashes' Code Red' or 'Red alert', it's time to get out of bed and get ready for action.

One common expression is 'timezone hopping' when a situation is developing in various regions in various time zones, and our operation takes advantage of the time difference.

A-Day or D-Day or H-Hour refers to Announcement Day, the day and the hour that the plan goes live.

Roger that: originally used during radio communications, it was confirmation that a message had been received and understood.

Aye Aye Captain: the expression originates from the navy and means 'yes I understand your order' and 'yes I will follow your order.'

To provide air cover: military aircraft would give aerial protection for ground forces against enemy air attacks. In a corporate setting, it refers to a team leader providing cover for the team to advance on their mission undisturbed by senior management or external influences.

Collateral damage: any death, injury, or other damage inflicted that is an incidental result of military operations. It usually refers to unintentional damage inflicted on an unintended target in the corporate world - a budget reassignment or redundancies, for example.

To hold the fort: a commander might decide to take some of his soldiers away from the fort to attack the enemy during a battle. However, he would need to leave some reliable soldiers to 'hold the fort' - defend the stronghold, if they were attacked while the commander was away. In a corporate setting, it can mean that a team leader is out of the office, and a second in command team member is assigned to respond to calls and emails and take over some projects temporarily.

FUBAR: fucked up beyond all recognition

Media Blackout: refers to the censorship of news related to a particular topic, principally in mass media. A media blackout may be voluntary or may be enforced by the government or state in some countries. In my corporate world, we use it to stop a news story on a specific topic to be published in any way.

Before you say anything to a reporter, make sure you are on the same page about what terms you agree to and what they mean and when they apply and when they do not.

On the record[29]: During an interview with a journalist, speakers can be named by the words they spoke. Everything in the conversation can be used and attributed to your source by name and job title. If no rules are set in advance, the assumption is that everything is on the record, including facial expressions such as eye-rolls and smiles.

Off the record: Nothing the source says during a discussion can be used in any way, shape, or form.

On background: usually means that a reporter can use the information you give them but cannot name or quote you directly. The reporter may describe the source by his/her position. Also referred to as 'not for attribution.' Remember that even if you're not explicitly identified, it still may be evident to the audience who the source was.

On deep background: a term commonly used by officials at the highest government levels who want to disclose information to the press without attribution. Such material can be published, provided there is no identification of the source or how the material was obtained—also referred to as 'no fingerprints.'

Chatham House Rule: in the UK, you often hear that a conference is 'held under the Chatham House Rule.' It means that the information disclosed during that conference may be reported by those present, but the source of that information may not be explicitly or

---

29 https://www.nytimes.com/series/understanding-the-times

implicitly identified. It is designed to increase openness of discussion.

Before you use any of these tactics, always bear in mind that none of these agreements are legally binding. It's an honor code built on the trust you and each reporter share. As a general rule, I would advise: 'If you don't want to see it in print, don't say it.'

Chapter 14

How to build a winning culture

"There once was a CEO who lived in an ivory tower, or rather a top floor glass office, working closely with her wise advisers, wondering why her company's results weren't as good as they should be and wondering why when she, on rare occasions, walked the floors, none of her employees spoke to her. When she eventually bowed to her advisers' pressure and spoke at the employee town hall, she asked why most employees peppered her with hostile questions. She answered defensively, the atmosphere turned tense, and she retreated into her office, shutting the door and wondering if it was her or them who were the problem. Unable to find the fault in her, she settled with them. She sighed, thinking - how can I turn this situation around? How do I get my employees to care more about the company they work at? Why are they not passionate about their jobs the same way I'm passionate about mine? Do I need to fire the lot and replace them with people who are better and more engaged?

Along came a corporate communications pro and spoke some much-needed truth. 'Dear CEO, the problem isn't you' she nodded. 'the problem isn't them' she frowned 'the problem is trust' she raised her eyebrows' And the lack of it. Let me help you build what is missing'.

The CEO put the comms person to the test 'show me what you've got,' she challenged. And a few months later, the tide turned. The employees started engaging more with her; internal surveys showed a positive turn on the trust figures. She felt more comfortable answering questions in a public forum. Productivity rose, and people greeted her as she walked past their desks. The CEO smiled, and they smiled back."

I was never much of a fairy tale kind of person, and as a working mother of two, I don't have much time to make up fabulously inspired stories, so I often hark back to my work experience to come up with these 'corporate fairytales.' But as outlandish as it may sound, there are some learnings in these fairytales and not just for the adults.

A few years back, I presented at an international communications convention in Berlin, and in one of the group exercises, the participants were asked to talk about their greatest communications challenge to date. I racked my brain as my peers told terrifying stories about media management of mergers and acquisitions, employee suicides, and complete system failures. As I stood up to speak, I wondered what I was going to say, and as the words left my mouth, the room started laughing, surprised. 'My biggest challenge to date was increasing the popularity of my CEO. He was new to his role and he came to me with a challenge - How can you make me more popular? I need people to trust me more' My peers laughed and agreed that that by far was the most unusual communications challenge and probably the most complex one to solve. How can trust be earned?

My background of years of observing group communication dynamics served me well when I joined a boardroom meeting that brought up the trust challenge. The management committee met up to discuss the company's recent results, which weren't as good as they were supposed to be.

One item on the agenda was to discuss a new communications strategy: how would those results be transparently presented to employees while keeping them motivated and encouraging them to improve their output. The tone of the message needs to be honest yet encouraging. The disappointing results couldn't be glossed over, but employees needed to be reassured that the company's leaders had confidence in their strategic direction and that with hard work, bold decision making, and dedication, the results over time would improve. The available options were to communicate in person at a town hall and respond to employees' questions in a live forum - a two-way communication process, as well as sending them a video message - a one-way communication process. There was some initial push back on the tone of the message, and the idea of novel transparency was met with skepticism as to how that thinking would increase trust and employee engagement.

When the news is challenging, employees need to hear from their leader directly. Employees shouldn't hear bad news from an outside source such as the media, for example, as it will only increase their mistrust and disconnect them from the shared company vision. It is necessary to be open with employees; give the context of the situation, explain the 'why' and how their leaders feel about it. It shouldn't be a blame-shifting attitude; it isn't an 'us' versus 'them' position. It is an acknowledgment of an issue and working collaboratively to resolve it. Crucially employees need to be given an insight into how the situation can be improved, how they can work more efficiently to get to a better outcome.

A small adjustment in tone and messaging can significantly and positively impact staff morale and encourage employees to improve collectively. The leadership team agreed to the change in style, and the communication was distributed to all employees. A short survey to gauge the impact of the message revealed that employees appreciated the open dialogue, the authenticity of the responses, and being given the information upfront. The most significant jump in the scores was the increase in trust. While employees didn't think positively about the firm's overall financial performance, they appreciated the reassurance that there was a confident strategy to improve, and they were given the confidence that if they worked as a team, the situation would improve over time.

From that moment on, something shifted in the senior leadership team's attitude towards their role. Leaders and managers started to embrace the dialogue with their teams, celebrate their success, and give honest feedback when things didn't go to plan. As a result of that shift in thinking, they moved communications to the top of their skill set list and engaged in two-way communications regularly, emphasizing blameless post-mortems - meetings in which the focus is on analyzing mistakes without blame and finding solutions.

We are often under the impression that we must obey specific leadership criteria when in a leadership role and must come across in a certain way. Be serious, be expectant, and assert your authority, resulting in coming across as detached, entitled, and self-serving.

Back in the corporate world of the 80s, it was all about running your team with an iron fist. There are persistent rumors in the financial industry that some companies operated a performance threshold to eliminate underperforming employees on an annual basis. If you fall below the set performance threshold, you get three warnings to better your results, and then if you don't, you are out. Teams are run competitively, and team spirit is a concept that doesn't work in an environment where everyone was trying to outdo each other to ensure they weren't in the bottom half of the team's performance.

In those days, one key incentive was monetary compensation, in a very 'every man for himself' kind of way. The more cut-throat you were, the more likely you were going to stand out from the crowd, and the more likely it would be that you were at the top of your bonus pool. Managers focused on weaknesses, and it was common practice to name and shame people's underperformance publicly as a deterrent to others. It was a tactic of fear and intimidation. It can be very effective, but to my mind, only in the short term. In today's corporate world, we have shifted our perception.

If you want the best out of people, you need to give them more than monetary compensation, more than performing well out of fear. Top performers no longer wish to work in a cut-throat and threatening environment; they want to be recognized for their skills, creativity, and individual input. They value collaboration and a common purpose.

In today's corporate environment, employees seek trust and a win-win relationship with their employer, under which employees provide skills that build businesses and employers offer experiences that build careers. It is changing the focus from the backward-looking annual review of 'what have you done for me' to the forward-looking productive conversation that asks 'how can you contribute to the company and how this benefits your career.' Talented individuals don't need or want lifetime employment - they have plenty of options and are attracted to leaders who help them realize their dreams. If you want them, make sure they want you too.

Leaders have the responsibility to change the approach they take to manage their teams. There are three main leadership styles: authoritarian, democratic, and laissez-faire.

As the sole decision-maker, an authoritarian leader will most likely adopt a leadership style with less input from the team. Creativity and innovation will probably be low as new ideas from the group will not be accepted unless coming from the leader. The level of micromanagement is likely to be high, and the team set up is very structured.

A democratic leader will not only accept but also encourage new ideas and innovative thinking. The democratic leader's management style will be more hands-off to allow team members to manage their workloads themselves. For individuals who need more guidance, usually the more junior team members, the hands-off approach can be challenging to adjust to.

A laissez-faire leader will have a completely hands-off approach and give team members complete freedom to achieve their goals. This approach generally works well with senior team members who appreciate the freedom to pursue their ideas and are highly motivated. However, productivity might not be as high as expected, and the results may vary and risk not being aligned with the company's priorities.

There isn't a leadership style that is better than another; rather, it is dependent on the team managed. Many leaders have an underlying management style, but those who are most effective in getting the best out of their people are those who can adapt their style to their employees. For example, a younger team member would generally need more guidance, and the authoritarian approach with structure might work more efficiently than a laissez-faire approach, which could lead to a lack of motivation, distraction, and not achieving the desired outcomes. However, a senior and independent employee will feel validated if given more freedom to manage their objectives. Overall a transparent and genuine approach motivates employees more than any 'smoke and mirror' approach reminiscent of a defunct management style.

To recap, here are the seven takeaways to build a winning corporate culture:

1. Lead from the top, lead by example

The same way children look to their parents to learn, assimilate, and mimic their behaviors, employees look to their leader to understand their role in the corporate hierarchy and their attitudes. The influence of leading by example is vital. A winning culture starts with the CEO and the executive committee; their behaviors and values will trickle down the hierarchy, influence middle management and, eventually, each employee. If you want your employees to become winners and live up to their full potential, you need to display the winning attitudes. Show that you are hardworking, that you are successful yourself. But by doing so, remember to remain humble and approachable. Employees appreciate a leader who isn't afraid to roll up their sleeves and contribute concretely to the company's objectives. Many will be impressed to hear that you bike to work instead of having a chauffeur driving you every day. Or that you sometimes eat in the staff canteen instead of quaffing champagne in expensive steakhouses.

There are many examples of tone-deaf mistakes CEOs have made. For example, the CEO of BP, Tony Hayward, was quoted saying, 'We're sorry for the massive disruption it's caused to their lives. No one wants this over more than I do. I want my life back'. He said this while boarding his sailing yacht, commenting on the oil spill disaster that claimed 11 lives and has since spewed 100million gallons of toxic oil into the Gulf of Mexico in 2010.

Or as my friend Claudine mentioned: 'Our CEO addressed his whole staff talking about the need for stronger cost-cutting measures following the coronavirus pandemic. And he filmed himself talking standing in front of his LA mansion, with a gigantic pool in the background. Talk about tone deaf!'.

Your employees need to see and hear that you are proud of the company you lead, you are passionate about your job, and the role the company plays in its industry and society as it will inspire them to adopt the same behaviors.

2. Communicate often, particularly in times of pressure

Senior managers often tend to communicate with their stakeholders more than with the employees reporting to them. However, employees need to hear from their leaders often; the visibility will not only reassure them that they are receiving the backing of their leader, but they will also appreciate the ability to ask questions, get guidance and crucially get feedback on their projects to progress and ultimately reach their objectives. Some leaders set up a weekly team meeting to discuss long-term projects, daily check-ins with the team to ensure questions can be answered and workloads can be shared or reallocated, and team events to foster a feeling of 'togetherness' to create strong bonds among team members. This is particularly relevant in times of pressure. The higher the pressure, the more visible management needs to be with their teams. Employees need to feel that their managers give them 'air cover' and 'have their backs.' In times of stress, leaders are expected to steady the nerves, reassure the course to take, and steer the team back into the right swim lanes. Leaders must not be defeatist as their pessimistic views will influence their employees; instead, a solutions-driven attitude will get everyone thinking about solutions and solve the problems at hand rather than resign themselves to failure. Leaders must, however, not gloss over the negative news. A negative situation can't be ignored and must be pragmatically taken head-on and then swiftly switch into solution seeking mode. Don't dwell on the negative. Acknowledge and then move to the part where everyone starts thinking about the answers.

3. Have a vision and strong values

People trust their leader to have a broad vision, a bigger picture, a purpose, and an objective to attain. If a leader doesn't have that or doesn't communicate that to employees, you run the risk of disengagement. As a leader, if you don't care about your company's future, why should your employees? Sure, they will work sufficiently to earn their paycheck, but they won't go above and beyond to find new ways of doing things, be more creative, or more effective. A leader's vision is what motivates employees to join in. It should be bold and game-changing. It should have a purpose to benefit accountability. A strong company vision statement will guide the company's philosophy and way of doing things and forge corporate personality. A vision statement for an organization focuses on the potential inherent in its future; it's about what they intend to be, what the company aspires to be. Not to be confused with the 'mission statement,' which is 'how' the company will execute on the vision statement, which is looking at answering the 'what' instead.

Some examples of strong company vision statements:

Apple Computer:

"We believe that we are on the face of the earth to make great products, and that's not changing. We are always focusing on innovating. We believe in the simple, not the complex. We believe that we need to own and control the primary technologies behind the products we make and participate only in markets to make a significant contribution.

We believe in saying no to thousands of projects to focus on the few that are truly important and meaningful to us. We believe in deep collaboration and cross-pollination of our groups, which allow us to innovate in a way that others cannot. And frankly, we don't settle for anything less than excellence in every group in the company, and we have the self-honesty to admit when we're wrong and the courage to change. And I think regardless of who is in what job, those values are so embedded in this company that Apple will do exceptionally well."

Tim Cook, CEO of Apple Computer[30]

Patagonia:

Build the best product
Our criteria for the best product rests on function, repairability, and, foremost, durability. Among the most direct ways, we can limit ecological impacts with goods that last for generations or can be recycled, so the materials in them remain in use—making the best product matters for saving the planet.

Cause no unnecessary harm
We know that our business activity - from lighting stores to dyeing shirts - is part of the problem. We work steadily to change our business practices and share what we've learned. But we recognize that this is not enough. We seek not only to do less harm but more good.

Use business to protect nature
The challenges we face as a society require leadership. Once we identify a problem, we act. We embrace risk and act to protect and restore the stability, integrity, and beauty of the web of life.

---

[30] as quoted in Business Insider

Not bound by convention
        Our success - and much of the fun - lies in
developing new ways to do things."
As stated on Patagonia.com

4.   Trust your employees with more autonomy

When I worked at a global financial institution many years ago, I remember working on a social media proposal. It involved allowing employees to become social media ambassadors, i.e., posting on their accounts on behalf of their company. The request was met with much skepticism. 'But what if employees post inappropriate content? We can't possibly monitor everyone's activities' there was much anxiety around giving employees that extra responsibility even after the promise of getting employees to sign up for training and compliance sessions. In my opinion, it was an unnecessary worry. Most employees will know their role and how to interact on social media when speaking on behalf of their company. The risk factor for someone to make a voluntary faux-pas is very low. Companies with strict hierarchies generally find it difficult to give more autonomy to employees. However, if you trust your employees with extra responsibility, it will encourage responsible behavior. With the appropriate briefing and preparation, employees will rise to the occasion. To improve engagement, give your employees more autonomy. Feeling trusted is invaluable, and your employees will not only complete their assigned tasks but go above and beyond their remit to ensure that the trust remains intact.

5. Communicate the wins

As a CEO or a manager, part of your role is to provide feedback on your employees' work. You are controlling the quality of the output, and you give guidance on how to improve. It is essential to create a virtuous circle of success by incentivizing employees to deliver to their best ability, by giving them a degree of autonomy to be creative and innovative, by playing back the team's success, the company or the individual. The majority of us want to do a good job, successfully tackle challenges, and achieve our goals. We also like to be recognized for the efforts we have put in. When done well, employee recognition schemes increase employee engagement. Success breeds success. Everyone wants to be part of a winning team. People gravitate to positive and inspiring people, and they want to emulate their accomplishments.

6.   Encourage life-long learning

It is in the interest of both the company and the employee to encourage employees to expand their skill sets. Be it to become a real expert in their field or to develop into adjacent expertise. The concept of life-long learning is designed to create a win-win scenario where both parties find an advantage in the arrangement. Managers need to encourage their employees to take courses to develop their skills in their roles, either broader subjects such as management skills, presentation, and negotiation skills or skills specific to their field. There are two ways to succeed in a corporate environment: either becoming a manager or becoming a real expert. Both options are equally rewarding but depend on people's preferences and working styles. Some people excel at managing others while becoming more hands-off, and some prefer to remain close to their profession and delve deeper into their knowledge. I remember a talented fixed-income fund manager, with years of experience under his belt being promoted to team leader. He held that role for about six months and then reverted to his role of fund manager. It looked like a demotion, and after a few glasses of wine at a dinner where I was seated next to him, I ventured the question. He laughed and answered genuinely: 'I didn't like being a manager of people, all the HR stuff, the feedback, the performance reviews - I realized I just wanted to manage the money my clients had entrusted in my care, and so I decided to take my old job back.'

7.   Fail fast and succeed in the long-term

The reason managers are generally skeptical of giving their employees more autonomy is the fear of failure. A lot of what holds us back, as employees or managers, is the fear of failing. If a company creates an environment where failure wasn't something to be ashamed of but instead viewed as a stepping stone to success, employees would feel much more empowered to take controlled risks. The key is to make failing an accepted step to reach success ultimately. The IT department in one of the companies I worked at regularly ran so-called Blameless Post Mortems. A postmortem brings teams together to take a more in-depth look at an incident, figure out what happened, why it happened, how the team responded, and what can be done to prevent repeat incidents and improve future responses. It's not an easy task, and it can feel alien for many to talk about a failure openly. However, I see this as an opportunity to push our egos aside and admit that none of us will ever fail and take steps to fix the issue. Most significant problems stem from the fact that an error was ignored or hidden and left to become worse or be repeated. Taking ownership is the key, the failure is acknowledged, the apology is sincere, and steps to remediate the issue are swiftly taken. Following the remediation, the team comes together to analyze errors made, and processes are amended to ensure that mistakes don't happen again in the future.

Chapter 15

Lessons learned from the global pandemic

I spent New Year's Eve with my husband and friends in a club in North London. I say club, but it was a warehouse, made from fine London brick, converted for the night. The theme of the night was gold. And we went full out, slapped ourselves in all the glitter and gold we could find, and sparkled our way through a heaving dance floor. Hundreds of revellers danced to the DJ's hip hop sounds. The dance floor was packed to the rafters; people were rubbing shoulders and shouting in each other's faces trying to communicate over the sound of the thumping bass. At the stroke of midnight, we cheered, clinking our champagne glasses, and hugged. And kissed. And hugged some more. Some of us got a little carried away, and there were reports of one of my friends engaging in a conversation with a pretty brunette at the bar while ordering a drink.

'One minute he was talking to me, the next I turned to him with our gin & tonics, and the guy is kissing this random girl,' my husband recounted with a grin.

Imagine that: Going to a club! Dancing with hundreds of other people in a confined space! Kissing! Hugging!

Little did we know how fast things were to change and how 2020 would take a very unexpected turn.

Fast forward about a month later, it was 5:30 p.m. on a Monday when I was asked to attend a meeting with our business continuity team. By then, we were all aware of a novel flu-like virus that had spread rather quickly in China. There were media reports written in an increasingly ominous tone reporting the spread of the virus in the North of Italy, and then day by day, new cases emerged. The death count was chilling, and there was an air of panicked certainty that the virus wasn't going to take long to cross the borders into the UK. My colleagues had already worked with our Asian offices for weeks as the virus had forced many employees to work from home. Our business continuity team had already taken sanitary measures to protect employees in the office. And yet, to me, it felt like a faraway problem; I thought at the time that the risk for the virus to cross borders to threaten our lifestyle was low. And now the situation was very different; with the infectious disease on our doorstep, we needed to act fast and ensure that our business would continue to deliver for its clients and ensure that our employees and their families would be safe.

We wrapped up the in-person meeting with a ready-for-action Covid Taskforce made of executive committee members, business continuity, facilities, technology, HR, and me, representing communications. We knew that we were going to be busy in the coming weeks, but I don't think at the time we realized quite how busy and how transformative this experience was going to be and what permanent impact it would have on the whole fabric of our company and its culture.

I attended many, many Covid Task Force meetings following that initial one. Within two weeks, we managed to coordinate with all business areas and moved nearly our entire employee base to work from home. We started by dividing up teams to limit cross-team contamination. We had to go over contingency plans as well as succession planning. Our planning meetings had a strange war room feel to them. It was incredibly daunting when I had to divide my role up and nominate my successors if I became a 'casualty' myself. Eventually, the senior leadership team gave over 95% of employees the orders to pack their belongings and set up their home offices. Those who needed to remain in the office as essential workers were given special authorization, and the teams in facilities worked around the clock to ensure they were kept as safe as possible in the office environment.

The first week at home was a bizarre one. Time seemed to move at a different pace entirely. First, I was excited to have more time at my disposal. Without the daily commute, I gained about an additional two hours per day. My initial enthusiasm waned a bit when I realized how much washing up three meals a day generated in my kitchen. I also soon realized that sharing my office with my husband was tough. Don't get me wrong, I love my husband to bits - and I can still say that even after living ten months of the pandemic in close quarters, but I discovered he is a very annoying colleague. He speaks a lot. He spends his entire day on the phone. He also speaks very loudly.

A week later, our kids were sent home from school with the brief not to return until the three-month national lockdown was over. Parents all over the country braced themselves and ordered an extra case of wine in their online delivery. I was terrified. How would it be possible to juggle parenthood, work, and on top of that, supervise remote school teachings? It turned out to be a nightmare. I was switching between work and mother mode ten times an hour, and my brain was exhausted.

It was hard to adjust. In the first days, I was desperate to keep busy; everything was timed. Breakfast at exactly 7:30. 8:30 Covid Taskforce call. Maths at 9:00. 09:30 zoom call with my team. French at 10:00 and a weekly status update meeting at 10:30 while grabbing a takeaway coffee at the local gas station while the kids trailed behind asking to go to the local playground. It was a constant back and forth. It was hard.

However, I realized that we weren't the only ones struggling. Everyone else was in the same boat, regardless of their job title and their salary, everyone was thrust into an unfamiliar situation and worrying about their kids or pets making a surprise appearance on their zoom calls. And that changed the mood completely. It isn't easy to describe the atmosphere of the first weeks, but it felt like everyone wanted to talk to each other. The fact that we weren't sharing the same office space anymore pushed everyone to want to speak to one another. I believe it was a form of reassurance. If I'm still here and they are still here, then we will be ok. And faced with a common threat, all employees felt the need to pull together more than they had ever done before.

When people find themselves in a crisis, they seek comfort in the crowd for reassurance and protection, to share a common experience. Many employees commented on this phenomenon. In the first days of lockdown, the volume of calls increased dramatically. IT teams had to work miracles and adapted office set ups to home offices pretty seamlessly considering the unprecedented circumstances. They increased internet bandwidth, hardware was being shipped to homes, and new tools were approved in record time. Various new communications channels were implemented in record time using collaboration tools like Zoom, Webex, Microsoft teams, Cisco Jabber, Slack, Trello, and the list goes on.

The usual sluggish approval processes were discarded and replaced by dynamic sign-offs on electronic documents. IT teams pushed out new system updates every week, and incredibly, the adoption rate of all the latest technologies was exponentially higher than before the pandemic. The crisis put a question mark on corporate rules that pertained to a workforce in an office environment. It forced the majority to rethink how they were doing business daily. It was a unique opportunity to press the reset button, part with old habits, and focus on new and more efficient ways to do our jobs.

For some, it was more challenging than for others. No doubt different people moved at different paces, but overall the majority adapted well to their new circumstances. The productivity didn't decrease; if anything, it was slightly up. Despite the upheaval, teams still delivered new projects, and on more than one occasion, the delivery was faster than anticipated. I tried to understand what the cause was, and the only explanation I could find was that people were more focused on their tasks. Being at home, operating in a vacuum, giving people only the opportunity to speak to those people who could advance the job they were focused on. When we are in an office environment, we often get distracted by our colleagues' conversations, particularly those who work in an open-plan office. People wander past your desk and stop by for impromptu discussions. Those 'water-cooler' moments don't exist in a remote working setting.

The other significant change I observed was around meetings. In a corporate setting, the main way decisions are made or ideas vetted are through meetings. The majority of the day is made of meetings, and the more senior you become, the more meetings you host or get invited to.

Virtual meetings are exhausting, particularly in the beginning, as our brains kept trying to read the physical cues of how our interaction impacted our listener. Our brains naturally listen to about 7% of what the speaker says, 38% to tone of voice, and 55% is the interpretation of body language[31]. Body language is a type of non-verbal communication in which physical behaviors,

---

[31] Neuro-linguistic programming (NLP) is a pseudoscientific approach to communication, personal development, and psychotherapy created by Richard Bandler and John Grinder in California, US, in the 1970s.

as opposed to words, are used to express or convey the information, such as facial expressions, body posture, gestures, eye movement, touch, and the use of space.

In a face-to-face setting, we pick up these cues automatically at very little expense of energy. However, on-screen, our brains don't adjust that quickly, and we are trying to read the body language of the speakers and the background of their home. What books have they got on the shelf? Do I like the painting on the wall? Is the person smiling because they agree, or are they just looking at themselves? All the while, we cast a critical eye over our own face talking back at us. We are easily distracted. Now imagine a call with 20 or more individuals simultaneously; I would argue that the energy spent on continuous interpretation is more significant than during usual in-person meetings.

That said, there are some advantages to holding virtual meetings. They are usually a lot shorter and take a fraction of the length spent on in-person meetings. We tend to go straight to the matter at hand instead of the usual polite introduction chit-chat, which traditionally characterizes in-person meetings. We go through the agenda more efficiently and allocate tasks more quickly. We also tend to be less late for the next meeting as we don't physically need to get to the meeting.

However, I did observe that the softer side of a meeting was missing, the additional exchange after the session officially ended. The parting words that give another dimension to the conversation were challenging to replicate in a virtual environment.

What compensated for the lack of familiarity was that most employees ditched the formal office wear and chose a more relaxed wardrobe. That change happened across the board. Senior leaders were spotted in polo shirts and weekend knits. Managers had kids' toys strewn across the floor, and pets regularly interrupted presentations. We all got a glimpse into the real lives of our colleagues. People asked about a photograph on the wall, introduced their partners on team calls, or took their team on a virtual tour through their house.

The boundaries between life at work and life at home blurred. The hierarchy flattened, and conversations became a lot more open and personal. In my opinion, the loss of the corporate persona brought many people closer together. Instead of being distracted by power plays and petty politics, you could feel a real sense of solidarity amongst all employees in the first weeks of the crisis.

To summarise, I wanted to leave you with five things I learned from the global pandemic, and I'd wish I'd known before being thrust into a crisis.

1.   Allocate your time more wisely

Saving time and reallocating it more wisely became a great way to become more efficient and carve out more time to spend with family or doing pleasurable activities, such as cooking, running, writing, or painting. Not having to commute to the office and back gave me an additional two hours a day that I was able to reinvest somewhere else. I started making better use of my time. I realized that only very few meetings need to be longer than 30minutes, and if planned well, with an agenda and clear actions for all participants, they were just as efficient as longer meetings used to be. I also reviewed which meetings I needed to be part of. If I had nothing to add to the agenda and didn't need to gather information, I would either decline or delegate the participation to someone in my team who would be better suited.

2.   Don't be afraid to adopt new technology

Bar a few early adopter enthusiasts, mainly the IT folks in a company; most don't appreciate changing the tools they use on a day-to-day basis. Many even describe themselves as technophobes. This shouldn't be the case. That attitude changed entirely at the start of the pandemic and found more and more enthusiasm from various senior leadership team members. Today, not a week goes by without a senior leader posting a comment on our new intranet's social site, issuing a new self-generated video, or publishing a podcast episode. New technology is worth close consideration, and our minds need to be open to accept progress and change. Yes, it's hard to learn a new skill or a new way of working with a new tool; however, this is where progress is ultimately made.

I grew up in France, and I recall using an electronic device called the Minitel. It was a French invention built in 1980 that was widely seen as the World Wide Web's predecessor. A videotex online service accessible through telephone lines, and was the world's most successful online service at the time. From its early days, you could make online purchases, make train reservations, check stock prices, search the telephone directory, have a mailbox and chat in a similar way to what is now made possible by the worldwide web. However, it took until 2012 for France Telecom to retire the system in favor of the internet's broad usage. I remember visiting a friend in Oslo back in 1997. I went for a tour of his university campus and was impressed by their study facilities: not only had every student access to a computer, but each of them also had their email addresses and unlimited access to the internet. A concept my university in France, needed a couple more years to implement. There had been a national reticence to adopt new technology, and every effort was made to cling to the old device before the technology gap with other countries became too wide.

3. Adapt to the new world

If a company doesn't adapt to changing circumstances, it will spell its own demise. On the flip side, if a business takes a change in its stride and adapts quicker than its competitor, it will take the lead. This is not just valid for companies but individuals as well.

'It is not the strongest species that survive, nor the most intelligent, but the ones most adaptable to change,' Charles Darwin.

The more rapid the pace of change, the more impactful the consequences of stubbornly sticking to old ways of doing things. My most hated sentence is 'but we have always done it this way,' if it worked yesterday, there is reason to believe it will work today. But having done it like that for years doesn't mean it is still valid and right.

'All is flux, nothing stays still - there is nothing permanent except change,' Heraclitus.

The global pandemic has been, in many ways, an accelerator of change and an opportunity to modernize and reinvent the way things are done. Adapting may be difficult, but it is not impossible. Keep nimble in your approach, question every action you take, and wonder whether there is a way to do the tasks better, faster, and at a lower cost.

4. Don't be afraid to change your habits

Like it or not, we are all hardwired to create routines for our day to day activities. We love nothing more than to create shortcuts and habits. It allows us not to worry about the smaller details, and it frees our minds on more significant issues. Whether the change involves habits, exercise, diets, or dependencies, changing behavior is one of the hardest things any of us will ever try to do. Change stresses us. Our survival instinct is activated when we find ourselves in an unfamiliar situation, and our brains generate all possible outcomes and consequences of the decision we need to take - as micro as they might be. Some sources suggest that an average person makes an astonishing 35,000 choices per day, each being evaluated for a positive, neutral, or negative outcome.

But it is not impossible to activate change for the long-term. First off, your motivation should come from a place of positiveness. Counter-intuitively, negative emotions such as shame, guilt, and fear are not effective catalysts for change. They might be the emotions that trigger the want for change, but they are not useful in making us stick to the new resolutions. Positive and self-edifying reasons are what you need to change a habit.

Further, do not attempt to change too much too quickly. Behavior change is a big thing, no matter the behavior, and it is rarely possible to take all of it on at once. We have to start somewhere and with measurable actions. Big and vague has to give way to small and specific - and realistic. Set yourself goals and objectives and reward yourself for sticking to them.

5. Don't forget to practice self-care

The pandemic forced most employees to work from home and, by doing so, blurred the lines between two worlds that usually have a commute time in between to separate them from each other. There has been much talk about mental well-being and the emotional consequences of working from home. Some of us are lucky enough to work from home in positive environments and have a partner, children, or pets. Some of us are lucky enough to have enough space to retreat and construct our corner.

For those who live alone, live in small flats, or have flatmates, lockdowns can be very tough on the overall well-being. That combined with continuous news coverage on the adverse developments of the situation, one can easily fall into the downward spiral trap. Looking after yourself will help reduce the risk of burnout or depression. Steps could include taking regular breaks from work, going for walks, or doing a sporting activity like running or yoga, eating well, and staying hydrated. Rewarding yourself with something you appreciate, a snack, or an episode of a series you enjoy. Stay in touch with your family and friends, albeit virtually. And most importantly, stay engaged with yourself, set yourself a project, a goal, an objective. Be it mastering a new skill, or completing a new project, having something to build towards in the long-term will give hope and reassurance that there is something more to the day-to-day slug.

Lastly, if you feel your mood drops consistently over a long time, consider seeking professional help. These days the mental health stigma has been much reduced, and thanks to awareness-raising campaigns, most understand that our mental health is just as important as our physical health. A psychologist or a behavioral therapist can provide professional guidance on what steps can be taken to improve your mental health.

Chapter 16

How to build healthy relationships at work

Over the summer, and in between lockdowns, I managed to catch up with Maria, a dear friend. She is about four years younger than me and works in a large corporation. We met up in her back garden, conscious of respecting the 2m social distancing rules. While our husbands were firing up the barbecue, we settled into our recliners and sipped on our white wine. As both of us are working mothers with two children, soon the conversation veered to our new working lives and how we coped with the remote working situation. We both agreed that while working from home had its advantages, there were still many drawbacks, mainly when the kids were off school and crowded the house.

I did mention that aside from the children's situation and the fact that none of us had contracted the disease, I had, by and large, found the experience not too traumatizing. Maria was of a different view. 'My manager is just terrible; we have not spoken for most of the past three months since we've gone into lockdown. He doesn't do team meetings and is lousy at giving feedback.' She was frustrated, and I was keen to find out more. It turned out she didn't have much respect for the man who led the team she was part of. She thought he was doing a lousy job and did not believe in him as a leader.

I listened while I sipped on my drink. It did occur to me that her comments sounded familiar.

'Maria, please don't take offence, but it seems that you have spoken to me about this topic before. And I don't mean this particular situation, didn't you have a similar story at your previous job, and even the one before that' she nodded hesitantly, 'maybe, the issue isn't your manager, maybe the issue is your mindset towards management in general.'

I could see how my comment set the cogs in motion in her mind. I asked for a few examples of her relationship with her manager. She mentioned that the last interaction they had been quite tense. Her workplace had advertised a new project involving research work on sustainability. My friend, being interested in developments to combat climate change and other environmental, societal, and governance topics, was keen to apply for the program, and so she did. She was successful and happily accepted the offer to be part of the new project. In her subsequent conversation with her manager, she presented him with the facts: she had been accepted onto the program, and she would dedicate part of her working time to the project. To her surprise, her manager didn't react as positively to the news as she had hoped.

I asked her why she thought that. 'I don't know; maybe he doesn't believe in this project, maybe he doesn't want me to succeed or thinks that I'm not clever enough. To be honest, he is never supportive of self-improvement of his team members. He's just not a good manager.'

'Did you have a conversation with him before applying for the project position?' I asked. She shook her head. 'No, I wasn't sure I would get in, and I wanted to spare myself the embarrassment in case I got rejected.'

'So this came to him as a surprise?'

She guessed so. I asked her to flip the narrative around and put herself into her manager's position. As a team leader, your objectives are to ensure that every team member performs the tasks they have been assigned to and delivering against your targets. As a manager, these are the responsibilities your own manager will feedback on when it is time for your annual review. As the international team manager, I have a straightforward rule to apply throughout everything I do: No Surprises. Stakeholder management is critical. People hate being surprised in a corporate environment, be it by a news story, an event, or a new development. People want to know the information before it is a determined fact. In my experience, it's not necessarily because they feel the need to contribute or give their opinion. It is mainly to have had the opportunity to voice their views should they have wanted to. Failing to share information with your key stakeholders ahead of the news being broadcasted to a wider audience gives the impression of isolated decision making, which by design doesn't work in a company environment that is all about collaboration across teams. It might seem frustrating to bring in other people to get a project through as it tends to delay decision making. However, good working relationships are built over the long-term for the long-term. Trust is built through transparency. Transparency is made through sharing information and allowing participants to feedback on the project and take some form of participation in it.

'You're saying that I should've told my boss about me applying for the program? But why, it's got nothing to do with him, it's a separate project.' Maria asked.

'It does impact him, as you are his employee. He will be worried about how the new project will impact your ability to deliver to your goals. He will be wondering what your motivations are and why you chose to do so. Also, isn't it just the polite thing to do?'

My friend conceded to that point but couldn't help pointing out that even so, she found it very difficult to interact with her manager as she fundamentally disliked him.

'Basically, you have two choices in the future: either you take steps to improve your relationship with your manager, or you decide to leave your job.'

She raised her eyebrows. 'Seems a bit drastic!'

'Well, your relationship with your manager is extremely important. It doesn't matter if you agree with all their working practices; at the end of the day, you report to them, and they hold the keys to your future advancements in the company. Their trust and support define the way you work, your success, and your mental well-being. A bad relationship with your team leaders can have very adverse effects on your confidence and happiness in the workplace. If the relationship is deeply flawed and not salvageable, I advise you to speak to your human resources department about changing teams or, failing that being a possibility, to look for another job. But in this case, I believe you need to tweak your mindset and to work on gaining your manager's trust.'

She was willing to give the relationship a go. I suggested that come Monday she should aim to speak to her manager as soon as possible. Ideally, in a face-to-face setting, but given the pandemic's social distancing rules, a phone call would work too. I suggested preparing her remarks in advance, coming into the meeting with a positive frame of mind, and starting the conversation with an apology. That it hadn't been her intention to withhold information from him regarding the program and explain the reasons for not coming to him initially, she would describe her motivations and what positive insights the program would bring and how her participation could benefit him and the rest of the team. She would reassure her manager that her focus will remain on her tasks at hand and ask how she could address his concerns. I challenged her to stay calm and solution-minded; this wasn't going to be a confrontational situation, but a mature and professional exchange.

About a month later, she gave me a call and declared that her relationship with her manager and the rest of the team had dramatically improved. While she still disagreed with a lot of the ways her manager ran his team, she had understood that there was more to gain if the relationship improved and if she played into the collaborative team spirit. She understood the long-term gains of a healthy working relationship and that most of the time, it wasn't necessary to win an argument for the sake of being right, but instead that a relationship of trust was more valuable.

I believe we always have a choice. Either we make an effort to build a stronger relationship by understanding the other individual's position and make concessions, or we decide that the incompatibility is too pronounced and that separate ways are to be taken to the benefit of all parties involved.

If you want to improve your professional relationships, here are four essential rules for having a healthy working relationship.

1. Communication, communication, communication

Most of the time, miscommunication or lack of communication is the reason why many relationships are conflicted, be it at work or in your personal life. Taking a step toward feeling secure enough to recognize your shortcomings and accept someone else's perspective will go a long way to improve a working relationship. Make an effort to communicate your feelings, concerns, and needs clearly. Stay objective, professional, and solution-oriented, avoid blame, angry confrontation, or dwelling on past mistakes. Communicate often and regularly. Set up recurring meetings or email status updates regularly. Always try to find a compromise that works for both parties, a win-win situation that will resolve the issues and benefit the parties involved. In chapter 7, we talked about our body language and the importance it carries in our communication: our brains listen to about 7% of what the speaker says, 38% to the tone of voice, and 55% is an interpretation of body language. Therefore make sure your body language and tone reflect the sentiment you want to convey in your discussions.

2. Honesty earns respect

Be engaged and show others that you are engaged. Show yourself in meetings, be prepared, give your opinion, support that of others, ask thoughtful questions, and be proactive. Don't blame others for mistakes; take ownership and responsibility if something didn't go to plan.

3. Build trust and show commitment

Deliver on your promises and always follow up with people. Give them advance notice and explain the rationale behind the concepts you are working on. Knowing the Why goes a long way to build understanding and trust. Be proactive and help where you can without being asked. Where possible, offer your knowledge and experience to help with your colleagues' work but ensure you are not spreading yourself too thinly and never attempt to take someone else's workloads (unless they agree to it).

4. Offer your support.

Make time for everybody, not just the senior stakeholders. Be positive and avoid gossip. Office politics is a by-product of living in a corporate setting and extremely hard to eradicate. Navigating those politics can be a minefield, and if played well can be career-enhancing; if poorly played, it can be career-limiting. Gossip is its malignant little sister. People find gossip a way to discredit some and to bond with others. It is potent and can end careers. However, it is always a double edged sword: the gossiper can quickly be on the receiving end and become the one being gossiped about. One way to avoid gossip is not to engage. How a large team works together and relates is complicated, and there is only damage to be done by getting too involved in gossip or politics. Don't risk disparaging someone by joining in a joke at someone else's expense and spoiling your reputation. The gossip will be about you before you know it, and it is hard to win back a tarnished reputation.

Hard work, honesty, and a positive professional attitude are traits that will take you a long way in your career. Don't forget to manage upwards and work continuously on having a good relationship with your manager. By respecting your colleagues and proving your value by offering your time, experience, and expertise, you can quickly build meaningful and lasting relationships at work.

Epilogue

I doubt my mother will introduce me correctly to her friends in the future, even after reading this book. Although she referred to me as a CEO advisor last time we spoke, and while that's still not entirely what I do, it is closer to reality than being described as a journalist. And perhaps she'll now have a better understanding of how communications impact our lives both at work and at the office and how miscommunications might be the real reason for getting stuck in a job and not being able to move on. A positive mindset can really change the way we see the world around us and give us the confidence to change to benefit ourselves and others.

In summary, these are the eight lessons I wish I could share with my younger self:

1. Take time to observe the people around you and figure out who the different actors are within the group. Figure out either how to better fit in by mirroring their communications codes or how to stand out by going against the grain.

2. But regardless of which way you decide to go, know that your differences are your strengths. Be respectful of your values and that of others. Seeing the world through a different lens will be an asset to your company.

3. Mental strength is vital as it dictates your overall well-being and how you interact with others. Know your stress limits and learn how to say no and to delegate. Practice self-care the same way as you would look after your body and seek professional help if needed.

4. Trust yourself first by building out your skills and your confidence. Earn people's trust by being authentic and hardworking. Take care not to erode your trust capital; it is your most valuable currency.

5. Be prepared for a crisis, and when it happens, stay calm and go through the plan step by step. Be efficient in your communications and keep focused on the essential and the solutions.

6. Lead by example: communicate often, particularly in times of pressure but also ensure you get equal airtime for achieved successes.

7. Learn to adapt to a new world every day. Don't be afraid to start over; be curious enough to continue expanding your skillset continuously.

8. If you feel well in yourself, your communications pattern changes - if you use confident and positive language, both verbal and physical, people around you will react to it positively.

I hope, you, dear reader, will find some of these insights useful and I wish you every success in your career as well as your personal life.

SJ.

Acknowledgments

When I look back at what I have experienced so far in my life, I can only thank those mentors who I have met throughout. Some taught me through love, others through pain, but I am grateful anyhow. This book is the result of experiences, studies, reflections, encounters, and mismatches. In the middle of a pandemic, in the most fortunate twist of fate, I met my co-author, SJ de Lagarde, and we decided to embark on this adventure to write a book at a distance. I thank her for having embraced this endeavor with such courage.

I am grateful to Michelle Prazeres and Jorge Tarquini, who guided me in my college days and today are generous professional colleagues. Even with limited time, they offered a sincere analysis of this book. The more time passes, the more I become convinced that knowledge without generosity is just vanity.

This book would not be a reality if it were not for the unconditional support of my companion, Timothée, who accompanied each stage of this project and who in recent years has been showing me, even if unconsciously, what a prosperous relationship is.

I am grateful to my father, who taught me to be persistent and to pursue my dreams. He always knew that I was born to be a journalist and writer. Dad, this book is for you!

Gabriela Glette

This book was created through the input, thoughts, and actions of so many people. I'm grateful for every encounter over the span of my career, even the challenging ones, as it contributed to my understanding of the various communications codes that have impacted my life and forged the person I am today.

My thanks go to professor Ben Shenoy who has trusted me so many times to guest speak at his corporate communications masters.

I have been inspired by many of my peers in and outside of my industry always to seek how to improve communications and share that knowledge. I was lucky to have had supportive colleagues and managers over the course of my fifteen year + career, who helped me identify and further impact positive communications.

I am grateful to have met my co-author Gabriela at the right time when we both wanted to share our knowledge and write a book. I still can't believe we managed to pull this off during a global pandemic, working miles apart from each other!

I am thankful for Tim de Lagarde's practical support in design, proofreading, and making the editing and publishing process possible.

A heartfelt thanks goes to my loving husband Jeremy, who has patiently fact-checked every part of this book and given me his unbiased opinion.

And last but not least, I want to thank my mother for teaching me to be patient, open-minded, and a passionate communicator. Mum, I hope you now understand a bit more about what I do for a living 😊, this book is dedicated to you.

SJ de Lagarde

Printed in Great Britain
by Amazon